Pot-Bellied Pigs
A Complete and Up-to-Date Guide

Approved by the A.S.P.C.A.

Dennis Kelsey-Wood

Published in association with T.F.H. Publications, Inc., the world's largest and most respected publisher of pet literature

Chelsea House Publishers
Philadelphia

Basic Domestic Pet Library
A Cat in the Family
Amphibians Today
Aquarium Beautiful
Choosing the Perfect Cat
Dog Obedience Training
Dogs: Selecting the Best Dog for You
Ferrets Today
Guppies Today
Hamsters Today
Housebreaking and Training Puppies
Iguanas in Your Home
Kingsnakes & Milk Snakes
Kittens Today
Lovebirds Today
Parakeets Today
Pot-bellied Pigs
Rabbits Today
Turtles Today

Publisher's Note: All of the photographs in this book have been coated with FOTOGLAZE™ finish, a special lamination that imparts a new dimension of colorful gloss to the photographs.

Reinforced Library Binding & Super-Highest Quality Boards

This edition © 1997 Chelsea House Publishers, a division of Main Line Book Company

© yearBOOKS, Inc.

1 3 5 7 9 8 6 4 2

Library of Congress Cataloging-in-Publication Data

Kelsey-Wood, Dennis.
    Pot-bellied pigs : a complete and up-to-date guide / Dennis Kelsey
 -Wood.
        p.   cm. -- (Basic domestic pet library)
    "Approved by the A.S.P.C.A."
    Includes index.
    ISBN 0-7910-4616-8
    1. Potbellied pigs as pets. I. American Society for the
Prevention of Cruelty to Animals. II. Title. III. Series.
SF393.P74K44   1997
636.4'85--dc21
                                              97-3624
                                                 CIP

POT-BELLIED PIGS

by Dennis Kelsey-Wood

A Quarterly

Photography: Isabelle Francais, Todd Kelly, Karen Taylor, and Vince Serbin.

yearBOOKS, INC.
Dr. Herbert R. Axelrod,
    Founder & Chairman
Neal Pronek
    Chief Editor

yearBOOKS are all photo composed, color separated, and designed on Scitex equipment in Neptune, N.J. with the following staff:

DIGITAL PRE-PRESS
    Michael L. Secord
        Supervisor
    Robert Onyrscuk
    Jose Reyes

COMPUTER ART
    Sherise Buhagiar
    Patti Escabi
    Sandra Taylor Gale
    Pat Marotta
    Joanne Muzyka

Advertising Sales
George Campbell
    Chief
Amy Manning
    Director
Jennifer Feidt
    Coordinator

©yearBOOKS,Inc.
1 TFH Plaza
Neptune, N.J. 07753
Completely
manufactured in
Neptune, N.J.
USA

As pot-bellied pigs have grown in popularity, so has the need for the latest information about properly caring for these miniature porcine pets. At first glance, some people are captivated simply by the cuteness of these little porkies. But they have numerous other qualities that recommend them as pets: they are intelligent and interesting and can be quite confiding in their human companions. Given proper care, the pet pot-belly can be a healthy, happy pet...and that's what this publication is all about.

ABOUT QUARTERLIES

T.F.H. quarterlies are published in both magazine format and normal book format, at different prices of course. The concept behind this type of publishing is getting the information to you as quickly and reasonably priced as possible. Magazine formats are accustomed to being produced in 30 days; books have almost no time limit. Thus our Quarterlies are published by our magazine staff.

CONTENTS

INTRODUCTION

Although the keeping of animals as pets in a domestic environment has been going on for a few thousand years, it has really exploded during the last two hundred. Over this period the social conditions in Western countries have improved at a tremendous rate. This has given the working masses more time and money to devote to leisure activities. Among these, the keeping of pets has become preeminent. From dogs to cats, small rodents to rabbits, to birds and fish as pets, animal lovers have continually sought more exotic creatures to care for.

Various animal species

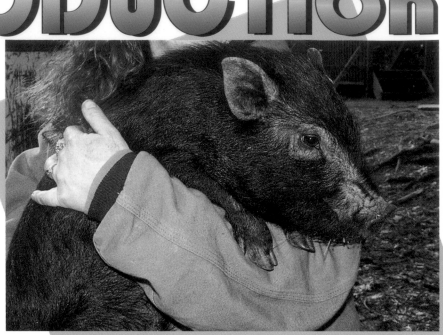

Pot-bellied pigs enjoy the attention and affection of their human companions.

A pot-bellied pig and its farmyard friends sharing a meal. Pot-bellies are one of the newer animals in the world of "miniature" pets.

have been the source of fads or crazes. Among these have been monkeys, apes, wild cats, foxes, spiders, stick insects, and more recently reptiles, especially the numerous snakes of the world. There has also been been a steady growth in the number of people desiring to keep miniature animals. In the late 1980's there arrived a very common animal wrapped up in an exotic package. This was the miniature Vietnamese pot-bellied pig. Within just a few years this unlikely candidate for sharing your home with has rocketed to pet stardom and is presently the most "in" pet you could buy.

When Keith Connell, a Canadian zoo director, imported sixteen unrelated pot-bellies into Canada during 1985 (two of the original eighteen not surviving the

journey or the quarantine period), little could he have realized just what an impact these were destined to have on the pet market. Intended as breeding stock to supply zoological gardens, they were to prove to be the foundation stock for the new pet on the block in the USA. In 1989, a second line of pot-bellies arrived in Texas. These were imported by Keith Leavitt from Europe. The vast majority of all registered pot-bellied pigs in the USA can be traced back to these two lines, known as the Connell and Lea lines. In more recent years there have been further importations from European stocks.

Unlike other exotic pets that have come and gone, either as a result of legislation being enacted that banned their being kept, or because they were too difficult to keep in a home, the pot-belly has all the attributes that should ensure it remains popular. Its small size, when compared to the average farmyard pig, is clearly the basis of its appeal. Miniature pigs (there are a number of other breeds that were established ahead of the pot-belly, but which have never gained popular pet status) stand at a maximum of 21 inches at the shoulder. They can be as small as 12 inches, with 14-18 inches being the typical size of a nice pig.

Pot-bellies have so much more going for them than just their small size. All pigs are highly intelligent creatures and they can be trained to almost the same degree as a dog. Naturally, their physical stature is such that they cannot do the same things as a canine, so all training must take this into account. They are extremely devoted companions that display the same virtues as any other intelligent animal.

Contrary to popular belief, pigs are not dirty animals. This image is strictly man made as a result of the unsuitable accommodations they are often forced to live in on backyard farms. On the other hand, one cannot in truth say that they are delicate and tidy when it comes to their feeding habits! They enjoy eating, which is reflected in the gusto with which they will attack their food dish.

In the short space of a few years the pot-belly hobby has expanded at quite a remarkable rate. There are official associations that control the registration of these pets, and there is a

highly organized show system. There are a number of obedience classes being organized so that porky will be disciplined in the niceties of living with us humans.

Other virtues of these pint-sized porcines is that they do not shed hair all over the place (the little they have they like to keep!) and they will not attract fleas. Their thick skin makes for a tough place for unwanted critters to hide and feed on. Pet pigs must be neutered or spayed: the result of this is that they are virtually odor free—as is their fecal matter. The benefits of pot-bellies can really add up.

This is not to say they are suited to every household, because like any pet you could name there are some drawbacks, few though these may be. Already you can read of pot-bellies being abandoned in parks. The fact that there are now a number of

established pig sanctuaries is testimony to the fact that a number of owners have experienced problems with them. However, in just about every one of these instances it was the owner, not the pig, that was at fault. They say ignorance is bliss, but this is hardly so where these pets are concerned—but it is a reality that through ignorance many people end up with a pet totally unsuited to them.

Having acquired your pot-belly, you should be able to look forward to as much as 15-20 years of devoted companionship from it. The actual longevity of these pets has yet to be firmly established as an average—no one has owned them that long as a pet! The age given is therefore an estimate based on both normal porcine age in other breeds, and from information, limited though it is, from zoological garden specimens.

Pot-bellies can vary greatly in their size and weight, depending upon their breeding and feeding. Some may weigh up to or even beyond 150 lbs.

SHOULD YOU OWN A PIG?

Caring for a pot-bellied pig is not something you should go ahead with unless you have applied a great deal of thought to the matter. While they may be compared with other popular pets in some ways, in others they are totally different. The most basic error that can be unwittingly made with these new pets is in respect to their initial purchase. It should never be assumed that all pets are suited to all households, and this is

A primary characteristic of the pot-bellied pig is its pot belly, which hangs low and may even touch the ground. Pot-bellies also have a swayed back.

There are a number of things that you should consider before purchasing a pot-bellied pig, including its suitability as a pet in your household. Whatever you do, do not purchase on impulse!

certainly true where pigs are concerned.

Just because your neighbor or friend extols the virtues of pot-bellies, you are better advised to concentrate your thoughts onto their negatives and their special needs. If you feel you can cope with these, then you will obviously enjoy the benefits of owning what is potentially a delightful pet. If you purchase a car, or any other manufactured item, it will not suffer if you neglect it. Only you will suffer because it may not function as it should, and will lose its resale value. But a pet is a living creature that is going to depend entirely on you for its future welfare, and thus happiness.

Every year millions of pets

are purchased on impulse because the owners simply did not give any real thought to what owning that pet entailed. They may purchase the pet for their children, or a relative, or they buy it because they like the idea of owning that particular animal. Many times a pet is purchased because it looks cute. The owner will not stop to think it will change dramatically as a pot-belly will within a matter of months. Often, the decision is made in total isolation of what their marital partner, or other family members, think about the matter. Some people purchase a pet for no other reason than the fact they have been told they can make some "real" money by breeding that pet.

In every one of these instances it is more probable than not that the owning experience will be a disaster, and the long term loser will be the pet that will lead a thoroughly miserable life. It is then sold, or in other ways removed from the household—assuming it has not died through lack of care. The first advice to you is do not take a selfish view of owning a pot-bellied pig. It is not only important that you consider its part in the relationship with you, but also the views of all other members in your family, and indeed those of your immediate neighbors who may suffer directly if you fail to meet your owner obligations. In the truest sense, the perfect pet owner is in fact a person who would dearly love to own a given animal, but who does not because, having pondered the responsibility needed for that particular pet, decides that he cannot in truth make the arrangement a totally satisfactory one for the pet itself. Instead they choose another pet more suited to their situation, and are able to care for it in such a way that it enjoys a very happy life. Such owners will be delighted with their pet, which will become an integral and cherished member of their family.

Introducing a new pet into your home can be broadly divided into two distinct areas. The first is in consideration of what owning it will entail, the second is with respect to its actual purchase.

Pot-bellies do best when they have access to an available yard or garden. They must have room to exercise.

TO OWN OR NOT TO OWN?

The Social Pig

Pigs are very gregarious animals, which is to say that they need to socialize with others of their own kind, with other species, with people, or a mixture of these. If this vital area of their needs is missing, they will become unhappy, moody and potentially very aggressive animals. If you cannot devote a reasonable amount of time to socializing with them, it would be better if you considered another pet.

Training is a Must

The fact that pigs are highly intelligent means that their training is a crucial need. Here it can be said that you must ponder whether you are capable of being a good trainer, and that you have the

Young pot-bellies are very cute; but when you are thinking about buying one, you should honestly consider whether you will be able to give all of the care and attention that it will need throughout its lifetime, which may well be up to around 20 years.

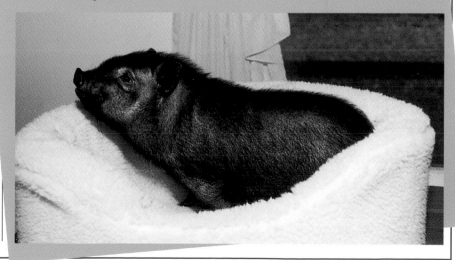

time to devote to this aspect of their management. The fact that there are so many unruly and dangerous dogs in any locality clearly shows that an ability to train an animal is well beyond the capabilities of many owners. It is not something every person should assume they are physically or mentally able to do.

An untrained pig can be a real burden on its owner. It will rip up clothes, carpets and furniture. It will defecate all over your home, and may charge at any person who it does not know, or whom it dislikes for any number of reasons. It will not hesitate to rummage through cupboards in order to satisfy its very healthy love of food items. In short, and especially in the home of softhearted people, it can make their lives a worry and a misery.

Nutrition

While a pig is not at all difficult to cater for in relation to its diet, it will entail more thought, and possibly more inconvenience, on its owner's behalf. Your local supermarket does not stock special pig diets as it does foods for your dog or cat. Your local pet shop will likely stock pig diets, so you will need to locate a suitable supplier and keep a stock on hand.

Home Sweet Home

Accommodations for a pet pig are not really a problem at all. However, if the pet is to spend some of its time outdoors, you will need to ponder a number of aspects that would not be considerations with most other pets. If you plan to

breed your pets, accept that they will not make suitable house pets. The sows will be much more moody, and less easily toilet trained, while the boars will carry a typical boar odor and may become more obstinate, perhaps aggressive, when there is a female in the vicinity.

Further, there will certainly be legal aspects to overcome if a breeding situation is planned. The type of home you live in should also be a factor in deciding if a pig really is suited to your situation. For example, if you live in an apartment, the number of difficulties you may need to overcome will most likely make a pig an unsuitable pet. For one thing, pigs cannot climb up and down stairs like a dog or cat. They also need a rooting box to forage in. No large pet should ever be confined into a home, and this is certainly the case with a pot-belly. If they do not have adequate exercise facilities they must be taken out for a good walk at least once every day. Given their limitations for stair climbing once they are fully mature, this might be a real headache for you. It often results in this need being neglected, which is the first stage of poor management. Pot-bellies are best kept where there is an available yard or garden, and of course they are ideally kept in rural areas where an exercise facility is no further than your back or front door.

Veterinary Costs

All pets should receive the protection of vaccines if these are available for that pet, but often these are neglected. You

cannot risk neglecting these where pigs are concerned. They may be a mandatory requirement in your locality, but in any case they should be regarded as an obligate need for a pet, along with hoof pairing (trimming) and regular attention to the tusks. The ongoing costs of attending to these matters is not prohibitive, but is obviously an extra cost when compared with those pets where these needs are not applicable.

Pigs and The Law

A very important aspect of pet pig ownership that you must address is their legal status in your immediate locality. At this time in their development as a domestic pet, the reality is that most local authorities do not regard them as pets, but as farm livestock, where they are classed as swine. This is not to say that miniature pigs are specifically classed as farm livestock, rather that they have no special classification. As members of the pig family they are therefore subject to all laws, federal and local, that are applicable to pigs.

They are subject to movement restrictions, which means that you cannot take your pet pig across state lines like you can your dog or cat. In order to do so you must have the correct paperwork relating to their having been tested negative for certain diseases, and that they have current vaccination and health certificates if these are required in the state you wish to enter. If you vacate a lot out of state you may need to consider boarding your pet with a suitable person or establishment that is able to look after these pets adequately, or to obtain the needed paperwork. Many owners ignore regulations but they risk fines.

If you plan to keep more than one pet pig, there may well be ordinances that stipulate the type of housing that must be supplied if it is kept outdoors. There will almost certainly be regulations in respect of how you will dispose of fecal matter, how near to residential homes the housing is, and that authorities must be notified in the event of certain illnesses or diseases. You may be prohibited from breeding in residential areas.

It may seem to you that the pot-belly is being unfairly dealt with in comparison to other pets, but you must appreciate that the economy of most countries is highly dependent on its livestock farming. Anything that could jeopardize this is a matter of national concern that will effect everybody in one way or another. To safeguard the meat supply, your government insists that the risk of disease spread within farm livestock is limited. If you kept a cow or a chicken as a pet, you would also be subject to all laws enacted to minimize the spread of disease across your country.

The Legal Pet Pig

The pot-belly that is kept as a single pet is most unlikely to ever come into contact with commercial herds, or to suffer from diseases that such herds are at risk to as a result of the very environment they are reared in. As a result, more and more local authorities are reviewing their ordinances

Pigs live to eat! This happy little porker is being rewarded for good behavior.

when the matter of pet pigs is brought to their attention.

In order to satisfy your town hall that the pig you are to keep as a pet is indeed a miniature porcine, many of the following may form part of legal requirements. It may need to be from proven registered stock. This will mean it has a pedigree that can establish it is indeed a Vietnamese pot-bellied (or other miniature) pig. There may be an upper size or weight limit applied to a pet as further proof that it is a miniature pig and not just a farmyard variety being kept as a pet. It will need to be neutered (male) or spayed (female), and its tusks may have to be surgically removed, not just trimmed. There will almost certainly be a limit to how many pigs can be kept in a single residential home, and breeding will definitely be forbidden in most urban areas.

Vaccinations will be required to be kept up to date, and permanent identification in the form of ear tags, tattoos or microchip implants may well be mandatory. You will be required to ensure that your pet cannot in any way damage the property of others in your area. This will entail fencing your yard and/or ensuring porky is always on a harness and lead when he or she exits from your home.

If you plan to breed pot-bellied pigs, the regulations you must comply with will be more numerous. With this in mind, it would be wise to make inquiries in advance so that you can ponder whether or not this would be a realistic possibility. You might need to relocate, which a number of people have done (after having gained experience with one or more pet pigs), in order to pursue their desire to become involved in the breeding side of the hobby.

SO WHAT'S THE GOOD NEWS?

If the text so far has not put you totally off the whole idea of owning a pot-bellied pig, you are either the sort of person who is never prepared to consider the problems, but only their own desire to own this or that pet, or you are satisfied that you can accept and overcome any problems, and will make a responsible owner. What then are the virtues of these diminutive porcines, and why have they attracted so much interest in such a short span of time?

Clearly, the fact that they are an unusual pet, verging on the exotic, has of itself been a factor in their rapid rise to great popularity. But the main reason they have made it as a house pet is because they possess most of the features that a pet needs if it is to be an integral member of a household. Their great intelligence means that they can be extremely confiding animals that will relate closely to their owners and anyone else who treats them with kindness. They can be very amusing in their antics, and they will happily get along with just about any other pet you might own. They are not predatory in nature, so make friends with the other animals whose home they may share. If they are neutered, they have no unpleasant odor.

While it cannot be honestly stated that their eating manners are beyond comment, this can be beneficial. The fact they will happily devour almost anything means you will always have something on hand with which to feed them should by chance you happen to run out of their regular porcine diet.

If they are properly trained to the home environment, you will find they are very clean animals. They are not noisy creatures, though should they have reason to squeal it is a sound that will carry, rather like the raucous voice of a medium to large parrot. But, this will only be so if they are frightened by something.

No pet should be purchased for its image appeal, but the reality is that when you take your little suid out for a walk, it will be the source of tremendous admiration and attention. Pigs are still not so well known that the average person knows much about them. Many owners have struck up lasting friendships as a result of an acquaintance prompted by their little piggy being taken for a stroll.

Taking an overview of the pot-bellied pig, you can see that it really is not so different from most other pets in the sense that there are undeniable drawbacks to its ownership, and these must be carefully balanced with its many and varied attributes.

The basic color of pot-bellies is black, but a number of other colors and color patterns are also available in the hobby.

CHOOSING A PET PIG

Once you have made the decision to purchase a pot-bellied pig you will no doubt want to obtain it as soon as possible. This could prove the first and most basic mistake you make. It could result in all of your hopes being dashed if you do not go about the process in the right manner. While this comment is true for any animal, it is especially so for a pig where there are so many considerations that do not apply to other pets you are likely to have purchased in the past.

All too often you can read about the heartache created when people have too readily parted with their cash without taking any precautions at all to ensure their investment, and any pet is an investment in one or more ways. It is so easy to go home with a little piglet that was just so cute you could not help but purchase it. In any case, the kids were wild about it so what could you do?

Well, I'll just bet you will be really wild if you later find it is not a genuine pot-belly and matures into an enormous monster that is so large and heavy it might just go crashing through your floorboards. Then what will happen to it, especially if the whole family loves it? It will certainly attract attention when it is taken out, so much so that your local town hall officials may slap you with a summons for keeping a farmyard pig! The sad truth is

If properly trained and socialized, a pot-bellied pig can be quite a companionable pet.

that the scenario described has already happened to many pet pig owners. Uncaring people have abandoned their pets in local parks, or in the countryside: some pets have even ended up as bacon.

Even if you are sold a genuine pot-belly you can still obtain a "lemon" for which you have paid an extraordinary amount. This is always the reality when you are dealing with a pet in which your heart may override your normal sound judgment, and your desire to obtain the pet quickly may do likewise. The first advice you really must heed is not to compromise on the advice that follows. If you do, and you get hoodwinked into purchasing a pet that does not meet your original expectations, you and only you are to blame.

Buying your first pet pot-

belly can be compared to purchasing a house or a used car, it ranks along with these as the most important purchase you are likely to make over any span of years. Do the job properly and you will have no regrets. There are many aspects to consider because it is such an important purchase for the whole family.

WHAT SORT OF PIG DO YOU WANT?

Your first consideration is to decide what sort of pig you wish to own. By this I mean is it to be a pet, a potential exhibition animal, or the basis of a future breeding herd? Of course, each of the last two types will no doubt be pets, but there will be a marked difference in the quality of these when compared to the average pet pig. This will have a profound effect upon the likely price you will have to pay. Even within potential exhibition or breeding stocks there will be a price difference, because obviously some pigs are better than others.

The main criteria of a pet pig is that it should be very healthy, be a typical example of the breed, and should have been carefully reared so that it will make the transition to your home with minimal problems. This aspect is extremely important because as a first-time owner the last thing you need is to experience problems. The pet piglet should have received ample handling so that it is not nervous when you obtain it, and will not squeal and run off at high speed every time you and family members approach it.

It will naturally be rather apprehensive the first day or two but this will recede thereafter. The piglet that has not been socialized to humans will take weeks of devoted care before it loses its nervousness. Some may never lose this trait, because to imprint any animal successfully on humans it must be socialized at an early age, on a day-to-day basis.

IS THE COLOR IMPORTANT?

Pot-bellied pigs are available in a range of colors and patterns. The color is only important if that one color or pattern appeals to you more than the others. Of itself, color has no bearing on either the quality or the disposition of the piglet; these traits are inherited completely independent of each other.

Unless you really are determined to obtain a particular color and/or pattern, you are better advised to concentrate on obtaining a piglet of sound health and breeding, and one which has a very stable temperament that reflects its breeding and the care lavished on it by the owner. This is the piglet that will prove to be by far the better pet.

WHICH SEX MAKES THE BEST PET?

The pragmatic answer to this is the one which receives the best upbringing. In other words, neither sex is superior to the other though each may display traits you would expect that sex to have. The fact that all pets should be neutered or spayed means that sex-limited traits are displayed at a much lower level. Boars are less aggressive and domineering, sows are less moody. The most influential factors will be just how well your pet is fed, cared for, housed, trained and loved. Both sexes respond equally to these influences and it is these that, in any pet, will determine its attitude to you and others.

WHAT AGE SHOULD A PET BE WHEN PURCHASED?

An ideal age to obtain a piglet would be when it is 10-14 weeks of age. Very young piglets can be notoriously difficult to cope with in respect of their eating habits, and they can suffer badly if they are relocated during this difficult period. By the time they have reached the recommended age they will be much more settled in every way. They will have been desexed, received all their needed vaccinations, will have been weaned a number of weeks previously, and will have been well socialized by the breeder. Chances are they will have been litter box trained, and have become familiar with a harness and lead.

With these matters all attended to this makes life so much easier for you. I cannot say you will experience no initial problems, but at least these should be minor when compared to the situation that could persist if you start with a piglet that is too young and has not received enough attention. A very common error, not just in pigs, but in most other pets, is that they are taken away from their mother and siblings too early. This invariably induces stress. In no time at all the youngsters are ill at the very age they are least able to fight off diseases, and in a home where the owners have little experience in coping with them.

HOW MUCH WILL A POT-BELLY COST?

The cost of breeding a litter of piglets, plus the vaccinations, neutering, socializing and feeding are considerable at this time. If you are looking for low grade show potential, expect to pay more. For worthwhile breeding stock, of sound rather than outstanding or proven merit, you will obviously have to pay more.

You are sensible enough to know that a car dealer cannot sell you a late model car, in sparkling condition, and with genuine low mileage, at a price that sounds ridiculously cheap. If he did, you would immediately be suspicious. Buying and selling livestock is no different yet many people do seem to think it is. They will go out hunting for a pet at a price that could not possibly reflect the reality of what costs are entailed in rearing a healthy, sound, and well balanced baby. Sure, very cheap piglets are to be had, but more often than not the buyer soon begins to find out just why the youngster was so cheap.

In order to establish what is the going rate, the **only** way to find out is to make contact with a number of reputable sellers and ask them — and I do stress reputable. Bargains in any sphere of life are of course to be had, but they are only genuine if they meet all of the needs of the buyer and are below the average price for such. The price itself is thus meaningless in isolation of what you expect from that "bargain." I should add that the same holds true at the upper price levels. The fact that you may part with a large sum of money does not ensure you will get either a quality piglet, or a healthy one. It merely increases the chances that this will be so.

As in all things where money is concerned, there are always those who either have a false notion of the value of the item they are selling, or are dishonest and always on the lookout for a beginner who they can con out of as much money as possible. Only your diligence will sort out the genuine from the disreputable, or those who live in fairy land with respect to the value of their stock (they are

When selecting a pot-belly, health and temperament are the most important qualities to consider. The color of the animal has no bearing on its disposition.

considered "kennel blind," meaning they never see the faults in their stock and genuinely believe it to be high grade, so charge accordingly).

THE GENUINE POT-BELLIED PIG

Many piglets are sold as genuine pot-bellies each year, and the buyers really have only themselves to blame if they end up with less than the genuine piglet. There are

basically two ways you can be sure you are not being sold a "counterfeit." The first is by looking at what is in front of you. The pot-belly must have a straight tail. If it is curly, this indicates a crossing, at the least, with a domestic pig breed. Do not be kidded otherwise on this point.

The pot-bellied youngster will have, albeit in a milder form, a potbelly. It will also have the typical wrinkled snout of this variety to a greater or lesser degree. Its ears will not be as large as those in domestic pig breeds. If you view enough babies, both in sellers' establishments, and via the photos in books or journals, you will have a firm mental picture as to what this breed looks like.

The second method of identification is via the paperwork that should come with the youngster. This will include a pedigree and a registration certificate. An unregistered piglet should still have a pedigree. The latter indicates its line of descent, which should be pot-bellied all the way back through each generation. You cannot assess the quality of the piglet from its pedigree as many people mistakenly believe. At best, it may suggest quality is possible. Any pedigree, to any animal, is only as good as the individual that bears it, a point would-be exhibitors and breeders should remember well. In other words, no matter how illustrious this piece of paper looks in respect of show winners on it, these are of no matter if the pig itself is only mediocre. A pedigree can be extremely valuable to a breeder if it is used wisely.

The registration paper is a document that confirms that one of the registration associations have checked the pedigree and confirm that the names on it are genuine pot-bellied pigs. Both the pedigree and the registration form will indicate on them the color, sex and age of the piglet, so these should of course be the same as the piglet you are looking at. Sadly, some people have forged these documents, so again you are back with the need to be very sure you are purchasing from a reputable source.

THE QUESTION OF SIZE

If the pig you purchase matures to be under 100 pounds and less than 21 inches (53 cm) at the shoulder, you have a miniature pig. Whether or not it is a Vietnamese pot-belly is another matter. At this time it does seem as though some sellers are trying to vie with each other in advertising that their stock is really diminutive. Clearly, a really tiny adult pig has more value to some people than to others.

Be aware that a claim can be made that is true, but very misleading. For example, a seller may state that a litter of piglets was bred from 9 or 10 inch parents. This may lead you to assume that the piglets will make very small adults, which may be just what you are wanting.

What the seller does not tell you is that the parents were immature when they were bred. Pot-bellied pigs can be sexually mature from about

Pot-bellies can be trained to a harness and lead. Such training should begin when the pet is a youngster.

the age of four months onwards. They will not be physically mature until they are in their second year (at the earliest), by which time they may have grown substantially.

Likewise, a piglet may be advertised as being bred from parents who were under 40 pounds as adults, or the piglet's weight might be quoted. Again, the parents

may not have been mature at the weight quoted. Worse still is the fact that some disreputable sellers will half starve their stock in order that its mature weight sounds such that it must be a small pig. They may do likewise to the piglets. What you get is potentially an extremely stunted piglet whose lack of nutrition as a baby can never be made up for in respect to bone conformation.

Most sellers are very genuine, so do not think that purchasing a pot-belly is a hotbed of deceit, high prices, false statements, and so on. If you are aware of all of the things that can happen, you are better able to recognize the signs of them when you begin your search for the perfect little porcine companion. If you weed out the dishonest, and those more concerned with price, size, color or whatever, you are then left with the genuine seller. You must know the one type to recognize and appreciate the other. So, do not be overly determined to obtain the tiniest pot-belly on record, because such a piglet just might come complete with many potential problems you had not envisaged.

My advice to the person who wants a small adult pig would be to view as many mature and healthy parents as they can, then take a baby from parents that are somewhat smaller than the average they have seen. I would never take from the tiniest parents, nor the smallest in a litter, if I was also concerned for good type and robust health. Choosing for an exaggeration of a feature, when compared to the mean average of the population, in any species, is best left for the experimental breeder who is prepared to have many failures before an objective is achieved.

WHERE TO PURCHASE

Any person who would sell a piglet at an open market or similar venue has little regard for the pets they are selling, so are not at all a reliable source. Their stock will be of mediocre to poor standard, and they are unnecessarily exposing it to stress and disease by taking it to such a place. The only dubious merit they could have would be related to low price. The risks are not worth it because a low price is of no value to you if the pet subsequently dies, or proves to be totally unsuitable.

A pet advertised in the local press is one up on those that have been placed into shelters, but it may still have one or more problems that the owner is unlikely to tell you about. It may have no pedigree and may not be registered. If it has both of these, you should still contact the registry to check on the validity of the papers, especially if it is at a price other than low. Mainly, such pets usually have some problem, so the owner will hardly be in a position to give you good advice on looking after these animals.

Pet shops can be very good. A reputable pet shop can take a lot of headaches out of the purchase. They will have checked on the paperwork, know the legal standing of the pet in their locality, and may have purchased the piglet from a very reputable source. They may be specializing a little in the pot-belly, and may have accessories and foods. If this is so, they will want to provide you with good service so they will receive your

Male pet pigs should be neutered, and female pet pigs should be spayed.

continued business, and your recommendations to other potential customers.

Pot-bellied pigs have straight tails. Any sign of curliness indicates cross-breeding to a farmyard variety of pig.

HOUSING

Regardless of whether you are purchasing a pet pot-belly, or intend to become a breeder, you should ensure that you have the needed accommodations in advance. The better prepared you are, the fewer problems you will be confronted with. This will result in a smoother transition to your home for porky.

HOUSING THE PET POT-BELLY

The ideal housing situation for a pet pot-bellied pig will be in a home that has a yard in which to exercise, forage, attend its toilet needs, and maybe also eat his or her meals as well. They can be so housed, but it does add to the problems that need to be overcome in respect to exercise and foraging, called rooting, which is an essential need for a porcine.

Your new pet is very easy to care for as far as its sleeping needs are concerned. It will be more than happy to lay right alongside you on your bed. It may need a little help getting onto this, initially by being lifted, and later via a little ramp. If this idea does not appeal to you, you could purchase a large wooden dog bed and line this with old blankets.

You might even fashion a special piggy bed if you are a handy carpenter. Be sure such a bed is large enough to accommodate your companion when he or she has fully matured. Pigs do not, of course, curl up like dogs or cats, so the bed must be a

Foraging is one of a pot-belly's favorite activities. This must be taken into account when planning accommodations for your pet.

little longer than porky. It must also be quite strong, not only to take the adult weight of your pet, but also to allow for the fact that a pig places all of its weight on its small hoofs. It should be low to the ground so it can be entered and left very easily.

An alternative to a solid bed would be something like a bean bag bed which will not only take the shape of your

piglet, but is also warm and easily cleaned if it has a loose cover. You could supply porky with a washable sleeping bag which pigs enjoy pushing themselves into. Even a large cardboard box suitably lined with blankets would make a comfortable bed for a piglet.

You may purchase a large carrying box to transport your piglet to the vet and other places: this may double as a bed while porky is small. You can purchase strong weldwire panels in a range of sizes and make a carry crate with the aid of a clip tool if you wish to keep costs down, and yet assemble a large carry crate.

One way or the other, a bed can be supplied in a wide range of forms. The essentials are low height, adequate space, comfort, and an ability to be regularly cleaned without any difficulty. If your home is not regulated with central heating, extra blankets or cushions should be supplied during the colder months. Piglets in particular are extremely prone to chills, just as are human babies. Indeed, as far as temperatures go you can compare your pet with yourself. The chances are that once it is an adult, if you are cold, so will be porky; when you are hot, your pet will be likewise.

INITIAL RESTRICTIONS

When you first bring your new pet home it would be unwise, for numerous reasons, to allow it the freedom of your house. Even if it is house trained this may be forgotten in the excitement and stress of the upheaval from its former home. Only if it is confined to a single room, such as the kitchen or a large bathroom, can you exercise control over where it might attend its toilet needs. Further, if it is limited in where it can run, it will get to know you quicker. It will not be running from one room to another squealing and trying to hide.

If it is at all possible, provide it with a baby play pen, or one that has been made for puppies. This could contain its feeding bowls, bed,

rooting and litter boxes—so be sure it is large enough. Again, such pens are not difficult to make by stapling weldwire onto a simple frame to form panels, then forming them into the required square or oblong using bolts, hinges, or other means that enable it to be quickly disassembled at your convenience.

LITTER BOX

If your piglet is to spend

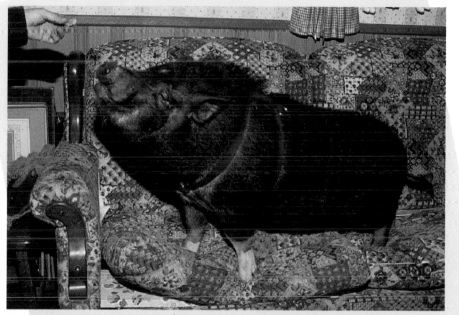

Establish house rules as soon as you bring your piggy home. If you are going to let your pet climb up on furniture, consider what the consequences may be when the youngster grows up to be a sizable adult.

most of its time in the confines of your home, you will need to provide a litter box of one sort or another. This may be a commercially made unit, or something you have put together yourself. Either way it must enable your pet to attend to its natural needs without any difficulties whatsoever. If there is but one problem with the size or design of the box (and later with its management),

you may expect considerably more difficulty in getting your piglet to use it on a regular basis.

A better way of relating the litter box to you is that it is no more than a particular area of your home where you accept that your pet must attend its needs. The box itself is merely a means of containing the fecal matter or urine. The pig relates the box to the area, thus goes there if it is so trained. In the wild it will attend its needs in a specific area if it is a resident in one locality, or anywhere if it is on the move.

The box must be larger than the piglet. One that is suitable for it as a youngster will not be so when it matures, unless the initial box was enormous. The width must be such that porky can turn around to exit without a problem. It must of course be at ground level, with a very small lip at the entrance that is just enough to retain the floor covering, but not so tall that it is likely to represent any form of obstacle to your pet.

The height of the side and end walls are not critical, only in that the smaller the box, the more important it becomes that the pig can turn around without bumping its snout on

Some pot-bellied pigs can be trained to use a litter box. It is very important that you change the litter on a regular basis.

the walls. You might initially purchase the largest cat litter tray you can find, then trim the height down on one wall otherwise it represents an obstacle to be stepped over. The floor covering can be sawdust, which has maximum absorbency, soil, shredded paper, granulated paper, wood shavings, or any mixture of these. Straw is a poor covering, while hay is only marginally better. Wood shavings over sawdust are probably the best option. These should be of a white wood rather than red or other colors, and you should ascertain that they have not been treated with chemicals. A few stones placed at the opposite end to the entrance will be helpful in that they may encourage your pet to move to this while attending its needs, it will root on these.

Although you may not give much thought to the size of a litter box, it is indeed important. If the box is inadequate, your pet will not use it, thus will attend its needs on the floor. If you do not have sufficient space for a generous litter box, then you

may have to accept the consequences of this. If these in turn are not acceptable to you, which would be the position for most owners, it begs the question of why you did not consider this before you purchased one of these pets. This is especially applicable to those with very small homes or apartments, and doubly so if there is no outside restricted exercise area.

Your pot-belly will appreciate blankets and other soft bedding material. When he is not sleeping on them, he may enjoy just rooting around in them.

OUTDOOR HOUSES AND FACILITIES

Whether your outdoor pet facility is to be purely an exercise area, an area with a shelter in it, or a total complex in which you can breed your pigs, it is essential that it be fenced in one form or another. Unless this is made your first priority, your pet will wander. You will need to keep porky away from your garden if you have one. If you do not, your valued flowers and vegetable crops will have a short life expectancy! While miniature pigs are not comparable to

their larger farmyard cousins in respect to the damage they might do to a lawn, it would be foolhardy to think they will not in some way damage a lawn if it is open to them. It is altogether better that they have their own area.

FENCE MATERIALS

The materials you use for fencing will be dictated by the extent of the perimeter or the environment in which you live. For example, the pet owner who is simply providing an outdoor facility will no doubt use wooden, metal or brick fencing that looks attractive, and can be painted in any color that seems appropriate. If the area is quite large, it may be more cost effective to use chain link fencing.

If you do plan to be a breeder and wish to allow your pigs pasture in which to forage, and have no previous fencing knowledge, the following will be useful to you. Fencing a pasture is costly. Much of that cost is in the time element. With this in mind you are strongly advised to use only the best materials from the outset. If barbed wire

Some hobbyists confine their pigs to one area of their home. Others let their pets roam freely throughout the house.

is the choice, do use the proper metal uprights for these and sink them into concrete at distances of no more than 12 feet apart (10 feet is better). The correct upright poles are notched to hold the wire. You can purchase retaining clips to ensure that the wire stays in position. By using the right materials you can obtain the needed tautness, and the fencing looks neater.

THE PET SHELTER

If your pet lives in your home, but you wish to provide him or her with an outdoor exercise area, be sure to include some form of shelter in this. The fierce midday rays of the sun are as damaging to your pet's skin as they are to yours, so a place to retreat from these is a must. The shelter need be no more than a simple wooden structure of a good size with an open front. It is best to erect this on a concrete floor so that it is easily cleaned. A layer of straw will make it a more comfortable place for your pet to recline. A breeder should also provide such a place for stock that is on pasture.

WADING POOL

If you really want to ensure that your pot-belly is comfortable during the warmer months of the year,

you should try and provide some sort of wading pool. This should be large enough for the pet to enter; a non-slip slope will make it easier for the pig to do so. The depth need only be 10 inches (25 cm) to allow porky to have a good wallow and keep cool. Like the litter box, it must be large enough for your pet to turn easily in it. Commercial wading pools are available from specialty pot-belly suppliers. It should be kept clean either by the

A pig that spends the majority of its time indoors will bond more closely with its owner than will one that is housed outdoors.

provision of a bottom drain, or by using a pump to regularly remove and replace the water.

BREEDING ACCOMMODATIONS

If you plan to become a breeder of pot-bellied pigs, you are strongly advised to prepare your accommodations well in advance of breeding operations. This might seem obvious yet many people become over eager to get started and do so without the needed preparatory work.

Alternatively, they erect make shift accommodations with the intention to improve this once they have some cash coming in from the offspring. Somehow things never quite work out as planned; the result is the typical pigsty set up that most people associate with these animals. The housing becomes a collection of lean-to sheds, a varied collection of chain link, chicken wire and old plank fencing, and an area of ground that looks as though the breeding herd was of 500 head, not just a few. It is a sea of mud and fecal matter, with a collection of old metal buckets, hose pipes, and half full bags of food dotted all over the place. It need not and should not be like this.

Plan and prepare the accommodations before breeding animals are obtained. It simply means you must exercise a little patience. Preparing accommodations is fun in itself and early preparation allows you to make detail changes before stock is introduced. Afterwards, time and costs may make such changes more difficult.

Planning

Always place your thoughts on paper in the form of reasonably detailed plan sketches that show the dimensions of buildings,

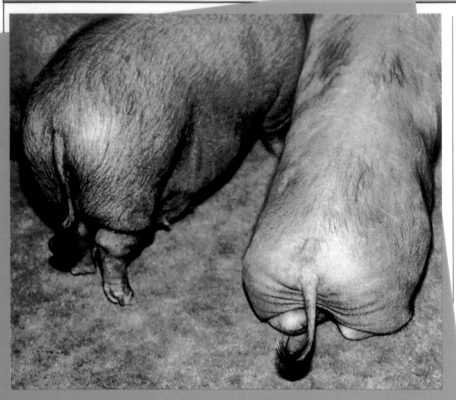

Rear view. A good specimen of a pot-bellied pig will have a full, level rump.

Try to locate buildings on the higher part of your land. Lower areas may be subject to flooding, or at least heavy soaking after rainfall.

Be sure that you obtain all building permits, and that all services provided to the breeding complex meet federal and state regulations with respect to the materials used and the way they are installed. Having lengths of wiring trailing across the floor or yard is not the way to provide safe electric to the housing. The sewage disposal system should be the subject of much thought if smells are to be kept to a minimum and meet obligatory ordinance requirements.

The Housing

The essentials of pot-belly housing are not really any

where the water, electric and sewage pipes will be situated. You will need to think in terms of having outdoor pens as well as maybe some pasture land. You will require an isolation building where sick stock can be housed, and maybe even a quarantine unit if you are likely to be steadily adding fresh stock while you build up your herd.

When planning to site buildings, ponder the known direction of cold winds, and have housing facing south whenever possible so it enjoys the benefit of the early morning sun. It is always better to have a food preparatory and storage area that is separate from the pig pens, even if it is in the same building, rather than having foods piled up near the pens.

Your pot-belly's outdoor recreation area must be securely fenced in to protect your pet from other stray animals and to prevent him from damaging neighboring property.

different than those needed for horses, cattle, dogs or birds. The accommodations must be light, airy, spacious, and designed so that routine jobs can be handled easily. The more difficult it is to do these jobs, the greater the chances they will be put off to another day that does not come around too often! Good ventilation is absolutely crucial to pigs, and indeed to any collection of animals living within shared accommodations. Many breeders do not provide this satisfactorily: by not doing so they dramatically increase the chances of disease becoming established, and rapidly spreading through the herd. Place ventilation ducts down low and high up in the building, and cover these with small mesh so that mice cannot enter. You should think in terms of one duct per pen. The ducts should have covers so they can be closed during the colder months, but some will be in use during these periods.

The ceiling height should be as high as you can afford to build, with a minimum of about 10 feet to allow for healthy fresh air. Supply a number of windows that can be opened during the warmer months. Skylights are very useful because they not only let in lots of light, but more rapidly release hot air, which of course rises to form a hot cushion above the window level. If heat is a problem in your area, you will need to fit ceiling fans, one or more swamp coolers, or some other means of assuring that the temperature does not rise to an uncomfortable and unhealthy level. On the other

Don't overdo it when giving your pet treat foods, or else you will wind up with a portly porker!

When letting your pig outdoors, remember that he will need a place to which he can retreat from the elements.

Above: *Example of a well-designed piggery. Note that it has been equipped with ramps, which facilitate the pig's walking from one level to another.*
Below: *This pot-belly comes and goes as he pleases. He simply noses open the door when he wants to go out.*

hand, pigs do not like to get too cold, so some background heating may be a necessity in your location. However, never allow the stock room to become too hot during the colder months. This will increase the risk of your pigs becoming chilled when they are let out to be exercised.

The floor of the stock building should be of concrete for practical management. It is easy to hose down and is cost effective to install. Place channels in it, or a very slight slope, so that hosed water is quickly removed from the pen. If the floor slopes, water should enter a gully connecting all the pens so it can be removed either at a terminal point, or via drains placed near to every so many pens.

Paths and a Shoot

Your entire breeding complex should be well covered with slabbed pathways so that you can move around it without wading through mud during inclement weather. Such a convenience will make life altogether more pleasant. It would also be useful to purchase, or erect, a loading shoot for mature pot-bellies that may be moved on a regular basis to shows or simply when you buy and sell stock. This unit enables the piggies to be walked into a station wagon, truck or pickup without the need to be straining yourself by manhandling them. It can either be a fixed unit at a given site, or be on wheels so it can be moved to wherever you need it.

FEEDING

Pigs are extremely easy pets to cater for in respect to their diet. Were this not so, they simply would not have become as popular as they are. The degree of popularity of any pet species is, in fact, a direct reflection of how easy it is to feed that species. I cannot think of a single exception to this general rule, but could name many desirable animals where their feeding difficulty alone is the sole reason they are restricted in the number of people who keep them.

The importance of correct feeding is critical in maintaining a healthy pet. The most recurring problem that breeders and vets encounter with some pet owners, especially beginners, is that the people seem unable to apply common sense to the feeding and other management aspects of their pets. Some owners are given bad advice when they purchase a pet. They then religiously follow this advice even though it is clearly obvious that it was wrong, or they may have misunderstood the original instructions. They do nothing about this situation until the poor animal is so ill they are almost forced to take it to the vet.

You can see this reality in the many half starved or obese pets that abound in any neighborhood. The first advice which you can rely 100% upon, is that the pet you see in front of you is the only ultimate guide as to whether or not it is being fed adequately. If it is, all other aspects of nutrition represent information that may be beneficial to you, or they are the opinion, and little else, of other people.

Rooting is inherent in the nature of the pig. If a pig is not allowed to enjoy this activity, it can become stressed.

The alimentary canal (digestive system) of a pig is not a precise machine. If it was, the pig as a species would no doubt have become extinct thousands of years ago. Its system was evolved to cope with a whole range of food items, some of which are readily available, and some which are less frequently encountered in its day-to-day lifestyle. If a food item is of low nutritional value, the pig will need a large quantity of it in order to meet its metabolic needs. If the food is of high content value, much less will be needed. The pig can survive at either extreme, but for optimum health the norm would be a food intake that represents a balance between these extremes.

THE HEALTHY PORCINE

It is clear that in order to assess whether or not a given species is being fed adequately, the owner must know what such a pet should look like at differing stages of its life. The more it moves away from what is normal, the more obvious it is that it is either not being fed correctly, or has a condition or disease that is preventing the food, even if this is sufficient for the normal animal, from being properly utilized in its body.

A young piglet should be well covered with a layer of fatty tissue, which is to say it will appear rotund or plump. You should not be able to see its ribs. When the ribs are felt they should have a reasonable amount of fat/muscle covering them. The area under the throat will be loose, but will have substance to it. A piglet will have a sway back and potbelly just like its parents, but not as exaggerated. Its back and flanks will be very well covered with fat and muscle. The skin will be supple, for it must accommodate the growing piglet. The jowls and face must be full, never obviously snippy, which suggest poor feeding or very poor breeding.

An obese piglet will have small folds on its body which are the result of excess fat. The snout should have wrinkles, but these should not be excessive. However, the extent of wrinkles may be more of an indication of the breeding line rather than the nutritional status of the piglet, so you must use body folds as more indicative of obesity.

As the piglet begins to mature it should retain its body bulk, never becoming skinny when viewed in profile or from above. One thing you should never see on this pet is bone structure, because this is a hefty pig. Bone must be felt, not seen. Obesity is seen in the adult by an excessively swayed back and exaggerated potbelly, as well as excessive body skin folds, including those at the root of the tail.

The general appearance of the eyes, hair and skin are

also useful indicators of good health. A sort of dull glazed look in the eyes clearly suggests something is amiss, as does hair that is very dry and is forever breaking. The skin of a pot-belly is normally dry, but not cracked and in obviously poor condition. It will tend, however, to become more dry and cracked looking in the very old pet. A well fed pet will be active.

Although pigs are famed for their liking of food, you can

A mother pig and her youngster. Pot-bellies that live in cold climates will need a bit more food than do those that live in warm climates.

still tell if it is getting enough by its demeanor. If it gobbles up everything as though it has never eaten before, and immediately looks at you for more food, the chances are it is not getting enough, and definitely is not if it is thin. A well fed piglet will eat with enthusiasm, but does have a limit to what it will consume at a single sitting. The minute it shows no interest in the

food that might be left in its dish, it has had enough.

If an animal suffers from lack of food as a youngster it can never make good its bone structure later in life, no matter how well cared for. Conversely, a youngster that may have been overfed a little can be slimmed down, and will develop into a super pet from a conformation viewpoint. A young animal that suffers badly from obesity can be adversely affected in that its bone structure can be damaged, as can the ligaments of the muscles which are subjected to undue stress because of the excessive weight being carried at the wrong age. But again, common sense must be used. If you see porky is getting too fat, he must be slimmed down before any damage is done. The main thing you should be watching for with any young animal is that it is getting enough food, never too little.

DAILY GROSS INTAKE

Another area of feeding that beginners often have difficulty with, is in deciding what the gross daily intake of a pet should be. They will read that at a given age a pet should need this or that amount, or that it should receive a given weight of food based on its own body weight. Both of these recommendations are based on sound theory, but they are only of value if a number of other factors are considered.

Very often the beginner does not consider, or even know of these other factors, so the advice is misused. The result is an under- or overfed pet. Let us therefore ponder each recommendation.

The first method takes no account of the fact that at a given age pets can range dramatically in size. One pot-belly might be 20 pounds while another may be 35 pounds. If both receive the same amount of food, the heavier one will obviously be underfed. Further, even if two youngsters are the same size they may differ greatly in their lifestyles. One may be really active and have access to outdoor facilities. It may have siblings to chase about and play with, or its owner may devote much time to entertaining it. The other pet may spend many hours alone with no one to play with. Clearly the active piglet will need more food in order to replace the body tissue "burned up" during exercise. It may require two or more times that eaten by an inactive piglet.

The second method takes no account of the fact that differing foods have differing "digestible" or metabolic values. It is thus only of merit when the food content values have been established, as in proprietary branded foods. Even then, consideration must be made to energy output levels. Further, proprietary food values are based on averages, and each piglet is not an average, but an individual. Some are able to

Pigs are omnivorous, which means that they will eat both plant and animal substances. Obesity can be a problem with these pets if they are not provided with a proper diet.

derive maximum benefit from the foods they eat, others have metabolisms that are not as efficient, so they need more food for a given activity level. The same facts are true of humans.

A RECOMMENDED REGIMEN

Taking all of the previous factors into account, you are better advised to base the needed daily intake on a method that will ensure your pet is never at risk of being underfed.

Feed a piglet under 14 weeks old four meals per day. Each meal should contain a mixture of foods such that it features items from each of the major food groups. Let your pet eat until it is satiated at each meal.

If two or three of the meals are branded mini pig diets, feed these as per the instructions (which are based on weight) but make the fourth meal a well rounded mixture of natural foods.

The mixed mash meal can be placed second or third in the sequence so as to provide a break from the "complete" diet. If the piglet is still hungry after the first meal, it will consume more when the mixed meal is provided. This might prompt you to adjust upwards the branded meal quantity.

As the weeks go by you may decide to remove one of the meals but, and this is most important, the gross quantity of the other three meals must be greater than was the previous amount over four meals. This is because your pet will be growing, so must steadily be receiving an increasing amount of food. By the time the pig is 12 months old it might only be receiving two meals per day, but these will be quite large.

Do bear in mind the fact that contrary to what some breeders are telling prospective buyers, a pot-bellied pig is not mature at 12 months of age. It may be well into its second year before it approaches full physical maturity. A boar may take until it is three or even four years old before it is fully grown. Once its height has peaked it will then fill out.

longer growing, to meet the needs of basic metabolism (heart, lungs etc), plus that needed to replace tissue oxidized during muscular activity, such as moving around or active exercise. You should also bear the following points in mind, and relate them to your particular pet.

1. A breeding boar, and more especially a sow, will have greater food needs than when they are not being bred. The sow's needs are variable during her breeding period.

2. A pig living in a cold climate will need more food

oxidized to provide energy while it was ill.

For all of the various reasons discussed you will appreciate that your pet's daily intake needs are quite individual to it, so what a friend's pet may or may not be consuming per day cannot be used as a guide to what yours will need. If your friend's pet is fit and healthy, and yours appears less than this, then of course you might gain from listening to him or her.

WATER

Before discussing essential food items, the importance of water must be stressed. Your pet's body is made up of about 70%, or more, of water. All foods, including dry ones, contain water in varying amounts, and water is also a by-product of body metabolism. The sum total of these still falls well short of what your pet will need. This means, even if it is given plenty of food items, such as vegetables and fruits which carry a high moisture content, it must still have daily access to fresh water. This becomes vital if the basic diet is of the complete dry type foods. Be sure the water is fresh by removing daily that still in the bowl and replenishing it.

Some hobbyists prefer to use gravity-fed water bottles because they prevent the water from being soiled by floor-covering material and bits of food.

The importance of this fact has a direct relationship to feeding. Until a pig matures physically, its food increase needs will steadily rise. Thereafter, daily intake needs will start to fall back until they reach maintenance levels. The latter term means the amount of food needed by any organism, once it is no

than one in a warm climate. A pig living in an unheated home during the winter months will normally consume rather more than its equivalent living under centrally heated conditions.

3. A pig recovering from an illness will need more food than normal, because it must replace tissue that was

THE MAJOR FOOD GROUPS

The essentials of a diet for any pet, be it a pig, a dog, a fish or a bird, are proteins, carbohydrates and fats. To these must be added vitamins and minerals. Vitamins and minerals are of course found naturally in the major food groups, and are the prime source of them for the well cared for pet.

Proteins

These are the most complex foods from a chemical viewpoint. Prime examples are all meats, be these from mammals, birds or fish. Proteins are also found in most plants, but in much smaller amounts. Certain proteins cannot be obtained from plant matter, which means that omnivores, such as pigs and humans, as well as carnivores, such as dogs and cats, can only obtain these from foods that are of animal origin. This is why it is very dangerous for vegetarians to try to make their dogs, cats and even pigs, vegetarians as well. These animals did not evolve to live on purely plant matter. They cannot efficiently digest it, nor absorb it into their bodies.

Carbohydrates

Examples are any cereal crops, such as wheat, maize, barley and their by-products, such as bread and cookies. Rice and spaghetti are also rich sources of carbohydrates, as are seeds, such as canary and millet. Again, most foods contain these sugar compounds in varying amounts. The value of carbohydrates is that they are the cheapest form of energy for an animal. They are therefore used to provide the maintenance energy of most popular pets. Even predatory species, such as dogs and cats, are given quantities of these compounds in branded foods in order to keep the costs at an affordable level. These foods provide your pig with bulk and roughage, but they also serve many functions in the overall metabolic processes.

Fats

Fat compounds are invariably found in association with proteins, as in meats, and seeds such as sunflower, safflower, hemp and most nuts. Butter, lard and many animal oils are rich in fat, some being almost exclusively composed of them. Fats provide insulation against the cold, as well as reserve sources of energy. In fact, they are the richest source of energy ahead of proteins. If an animal is underfed, it will breakdown its fat to create basic sugars, which are then oxidized to release their oxygen content, which provides energy. Once fat reserves are used up, the animal will then break down its protein, such as muscles, to create energy, which is why an animal will get thinner if it is not given sufficient food.

Vitamins

Vitamin compounds are not foods but are contained in them. There are many known vitamins. Their richest sources are fresh fruits, green plant matter, certain animal organs (such as the liver), and many fish and plant oils (such as cod liver oil). When a given vitamin is missing in the diet, its effect is always negative. It may result in poor vision, lack of vitality, reduced breeding capacity, poor growth, lack of resistance to disease, and many other problems. Vitamins are not only required in given quantities, but also in given ratios to other vitamins and minerals. Sometimes an excess does not harm the animal; the excess is removed from the body in fecal matter or urine.

However, in other cases it will adversely affect the way in

This pot-belly spends the better part of the day outdoors. A pig that gets plenty of exercise will need more food than one that is sedentary.

which another vitamin or mineral can function, and problems then arise. The ad lib use of supplementary vitamins can be potentially dangerous in a healthy pet. Only a vet can really determine if a given vitamin is needed in extra amounts. It may be necessary after certain treatments, because the medicine may destroy bacteria that are helpful in synthesizing certain vitamins in the stomach of the pig. In other instances, the pet may have been fed a restricted diet that has created a vitamin deficiency.

Minerals

Minerals are elements, such as iron, copper, calcium, iodine, potassium and manganese, to name a few. Their role is in cellular structure and rigidity, production of milk, and countless chemical reactions that are continuous in the body. They are found in all food items. Some, such as calcium, potassium and magnesium are required in larger quantities than others. Some, such as selenium, have been found to be of great importance to pigs, so are carefully added to prepared diets. If your pet receives a balanced and varied diet, it is unlikely that it would suffer from a lack of any minerals.

PROVIDING THE ESSENTIAL FOODS

Having established what the important food groups are comprised of, and what their role in the body is, we can now consider how best to supply them to our pets. The most convenient way is to feed one of the commercially made

miniature pig diets. Indeed, you could rear porky totally on these, and some breeders do, but I would never recommend this for a number of reasons.

First, there is the matter of pellets being a very boring food. A scientist can say that a "complete" diet food will meet all the metabolic needs of a given species, and I would still remain unconvinced. This would indicate that scientists knew everything about nutrition. Clearly they do not, based on all the contradictory opinions expressed about human foods, which after all are subject to more research than any animal food.

If it can bolt down enough food to meet its metabolic needs in seconds, something becomes missing psychologically in its mind. It does not consciously think about this, no more than a caged animal that has never been given freedom thinks about that situation. It simply has an inner urge to be free. Developed behavior patterns, such as pacing, indicate how caging dramatically effects an animal. Feeding can be compared to this from a psychological viewpoint.

The freedom to exercise individual taste preferences is denied to an animal on a complete diet, as is the ability to select from different textures (levels of hardness). It has been found that selenium and vitamin E are especially important to miniature pigs. Prior to this fact being established, "complete" diets were formulated for pigs without fortification of these compounds.

By supplying a range of natural foods you ensure that you are meeting all of the

psychological needs of your pet, while insuring that every food constituent, known to humans or not, is probably being supplied via the variety offered.

NATURAL FOODS

The range of natural foods that you can safely give to your porcine is so extensive that it would be easier to note the items that it should not be given. Even so, a few beneficial foods should be mentioned, which will no doubt always be in your kitchen at one time or another. Carrots are an excellent source of carotene (vitamin A), spinach is rich in iron, soybean is a good source of vegetable proteins, as are most nuts. Beet tops have a good vitamin A content, though dandelion is ahead of most plants for this vitamin. Dried lentils and unripe peas are a good source of vitamin B, while kidney beans have good carbohydrate and protein content.

Broccoli and celery can be recommended, while lettuce is 95% water and has little nutritional value. Cress is an excellent plant, while boiled potatoes and root crops, such as turnip, swede, marrow and their like will provide fiber and bulk to foods. Most fruits have high vitamin content so should be included. Apples are a perennial favorite, but grapes, apricots, cherry, plum and even bananas, can all be offered to see which tempt porky's palate.

Toasted or baked bread will give your pet something to munch on. Any cereal crops will be eaten, but bear in mind these have a high carbohydrate content so can be fattening if given in excess, especially if formulated diets are the basis of the feeding regimen. The same is true of your pizza and other Italian food leftovers. Butter has a high fat content (about 81%) so take care with this. Lard is 99% fat. Peanut butter is a good supplement. Cheese, raw egg and various milks, are good sources of protein, fat and calcium. Raw egg yolk is a fine source of vitamins of the B complex group.

Do not overlook wild plants and grasses. Hay is a great source of fiber and can be given almost ad lib. Most flower heads will be taken with relish. Never feed any plants that are grown from bulbs, and always check the poison status of wild plants. All vegetables and plants should be rinsed with water before being given to your pet.

Apart from offering any foods as individual items, you can mix them all together as a salad, or as a moist or dry mash. Porky will be delighted with this sort of meal because he or she can forage over these and will enjoy rooting out the favored items first. You can include bits of meat, fish or fishmeal, and meat extracts, each of which will provide needed amino acids— the precursors of proteins.

FEEDING MISCONCEPTIONS

The final subject that is worthy of mention is that of a pig's size, and feeding misconceptions related to this. Each pig is born with a genetic potential for its size. By feeding it excessively you will achieve two things. It will attain a size close to its theoretical potential, but it will never exceed this. It will

also have a girth that is decidedly unhealthy. The reverse is equally true, and more appropriate to what is happening in pet pigs today.

Underfeeding a pet will not necessarily make it small. Its genetic potential will not be reached. If it is small as a result, this will be because its growth is stunted, its bones malformed. It will be unhealthy and a poor example of the breed. However, such a condition, and any smallness

created by stunted growth, will have been caused by the environment (feeding, poor care and so on), not genetic factors. This means that even if such a poor specimen was able to have any offspring, they would grow to a size that reflected the genes for the size they inherited. Feeding, whether excessively or inadequately, will not effect onward breeding potential in respect of the genes that determine size.

Pigs love food. Coping with a picky eater will not be one of your problems as a pig owner.

PREPARING FOR YOUR PIGLET

Part of the excitement of having a little piglet arrive in your home will be in preparing for the big day. It is always best to have all the things you need in advance as this allows you plenty of time to shop around. You can get exactly what you want, rather than just what is available on short notice. Other than actual items that are purchased, the other part of being ready is in ensuring there are no dangers in your home for a piglet.

POTENTIAL DANGERS & DIFFICULTIES

Every home is a unique structure and some present more problems, and contain more potential dangers, than others. Before your new pet arrives, make notes on possible dangers. Ponder how you can best remove or at least minimize these. As with most accidents, if things go wrong it will be with some problem you had been meaning to attend to. After recognizing a hazard, do not leave it in the "to be attended" column. Fix it—that will be an end to it. The following are but a few potential hazards that you should look into with respect to your particular home. Some are constant dangers that can only be overcome by continually being aware of them.

1. Many homes have polished wooden or tiled floors. These can be very dangerous to most animals, including the owners. They are especially so for a hoofed creature whose little "trotters" have virtually no powers of grip on smooth surfaces. You can overcome the problem by fitting carpets if your pet will be allowed into any such room. Be careful that if you fit rugs that these are not prone to "skating."

2. In open plan kitchen living area configurations, a tiny piglet under your feet can be dangerous to you and itself. You may not notice porky standing behind you as you turn with a boiling kettle or saucepan of water. Piggies just love kitchen areas because they know this is the food depot. You might consider erecting a temporary barrier, such as a small gate, just while your pet is small, nimble and mischievous.

3. Trailing electrical wires that are plugged into live sockets could be dangerous to a piglet. Many nibble on everything to see if it is edible.

4. It would be wise to move all indoor plants out of porky's reach, regardless of whether or not they might be poisonous. In fact, anything that is small and remotely of appeal to your pet as a food item is best placed in a safe place.

5. If you leave porky alone in your home for any length of time, be sure cupboards are securely fastened. Their curiosity knows no bounds: their goal in life is forever to track down food items. If a tin of black shoe polish looks to them like food they will try to taste it! If you cannot secure cupboards from a very effective snout, the option is to secure the snout. Place porky into a room where he or she can do no damage while you are out.

6. Be sure balconies, decks and steep stairs are safeguarded so there is no risk that your pet might fall from them or down them. A temporary fitting, such as weld wire or a gate, will provide the needed security just until your piglet is mature enough to be safe. Although pigs are competent swimmers they might not be able to clamber out of a pond or swimming pool, so fence these so they are not accessible to your porcine.

7. Check that there is no flooring that has holes in it which might be a source of injury to a little piglet if it placed its foot in it. Pigs are actually very wary of such things but could be injured if they were to run in momentary fear from something.

8. Always take great care to protect against temporary dangers. Examples would be a trailing wire from a hot iron that you might leave in order to answer the door or the phone. If your pet pulled on this, it could be badly injured by the iron. Open doors and windows are another

temporary hazard. A door might slam shut and injure your piglet. Never leave power tools on, or even plugged in, if you leave a room in which there is a little piglet.

It is a good idea to walk around your home and consider what its hazards are. You might be surprised to find there are more things in need of attention than you realized—and not just for porky's safety, but for that of the entire family.

ESSENTIALS AND OTHER ITEMS

From a situation just a few years ago when pot-bellied pig owners had to make do with whatever items they could utilize from other pets, the hobby has expanded enormously. Today, owners can select from a growing list of products that have been developed specifically for these pets. Some can be regarded as essential. There are still some items that you may need to fashion yourself to get the ideal product. The following are some suggestions.

Rooting Box

This is an absolutely essential item for a pet pig living in a home environment. It allows the pet to fulfill a very basic instinct, which is to forage for food. If no box is provided, your pet will fulfill this urge on cushions, furniture, even carpets. A rooting box must be of a size that allows the pig to move into it and out again, with ease—just as with the litter box. In the box you place an

A harness and lead is a must for every new pig owner. Pet shops stock a variety of them that are suitable for pigs.

assortment of pebbles and stones on a soil or pine shaving base. You can include clumps of grass if you wish, and even sprinkle some of porky's diet pellets among the stones. Your pet will spend quite a lot of time going in and out of its rooting box to search for little food treats. This will make him a very contented little porcine. Once mature

you will of course need to supply a rather larger box which can be located in its outdoor pen.

Harness and Lead

These are other items on the "must have" list. The harness needs to be one designed for piglets, whose chest, abdomen and girth measurements are very different from those of dogs. There are three styles to choose from, but each have their devotees. The important thing is that it is a comfortable fit, and that it is sewn rather than riveted at its main stress points. The clasp to take the lead should also be very strong. The same applies to the lead which should have good width and be 6 feet minimum in length. Nylon is a popular material, but quality leather is always hard to beat. The harness can be obtained from specialist suppliers if your local pet store does not yet carry a range of pot-belly accessories.

Feeding Bowls

You will need one or two

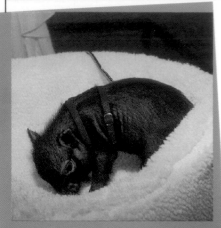

This piglet is investigating its new bed. Like many other kinds of pets, pot-bellies need a comfortable place in which to sleep.

Grooming Aids

Pigs have only minimal hair so they are very easy to keep tidy. A soft to medium bristle brush will be the only needed tool, to which you can add a few pieces of silk cloth to "polish" your pet. There are many products, such as skin conditions and shampoos, now available for piglets, but these are not essential if porky is in good health.

A tub of hoof conditioner is, however, recommended to ensure this appendage is kept in fine condition. It does not have to be one marketed for miniature pigs. Even grease smeared periodically on the hoof will keep it healthy and supple. You may find it beneficial to purchase one or more hoof tools so that you can trim and file the hoofs in order that they remain at the required length.

A mist spray bottle will be useful and can contain just

water, glycerin and water, or any of the "skin lotions" made for those who exhibit their pigs. A regular mist spray with tepid water will help keep your pet's skin moist, because this can become rather dry if the pet spends most of its time indoors. However, always remember that skin condition comes from within, via good nutrition, rather than from lotions placed onto its surface. If greasy conditioners are used, these will tend to pick up dirt and leave stains on your chairs, so select only those beauty aids that avoid this happening.

First Aid Box

If you do not already have a first aid box in your home, maybe the arrival of a piglet will prompt you to get one. It should contain the usual items, such as surgical scissors, bandages, antiseptic lotions or powders, forceps,

bowls for piggy's food, and one for water. It really matters not whether these are made for pigs, dogs, or any other animal as long as they suit the need. I prefer heavy crock feeding dishes simply because pigs have a habit of using an empty dish made of plastic or aluminum as a toy to be thrown about, often when the dish still has some food or water in it.

Kitchen baking trays make fine feeders as they are large, yet do not have high sides to them. If one of these is placed into a homemade wooden frame, it will not skate across the floor with your pet pushing it as it feeds. Breeders can of course purchase small farmyard type feeder troughs. Have one dish for pellet foods and one for fresh foods and mashes. A breeder might find it more convenient to purchase, or make, an automatic water system if a lot of pigs are in the herd. These are not costly to install and can save quite of lot of time.

Pigs are very attentive pets, which is important when it comes to training them.

swabs, cotton wool buds, and coagulants, such as iodine or a styptic pencil, to stop minor blood flows. It can also contain lotions for tummy upsets, as well as worming tablets or liquids.

Toys

There is no need to purchase squeaky plastic toys for your piglet as there are plenty of alternatives that are both safer and will be thoroughly enjoyed. A pile of newspapers will amuse a piglet for ages, as will cardboard boxes that can be rummaged through and flung about your neat and tidy home! A piglet will happily push around a number of scatter cushions, and of course its rooting box is really both an essential and a toy.

Pigs will enjoy chewing on short branches of fruit trees. As they get older, they can amuse themselves with an old rubber tire or inner tube. Nylaballs® are quite safe, but avoid any commercial toy that is easily broken into pieces. This especially applies to those made of thin plastic. If bits are swallowed, they could cause an internal blockage. One of the large Nylabones® is fine. It is better they chew on this than get into the habit of playing with your slippers or shoes, which will not be as amusing when they are mature and continue to do the same thing.

Breeder Items

The breeder will need a range of items that will be useful at one time or another. These will include a farrowing pen if possible, baby bottle feeders and syringes, a range of piglet feeding supplements, and maybe even special tooth pliers for the needle sharp teeth of small piglets. These items will probably only be available from veterinary or specialty hobby suppliers.

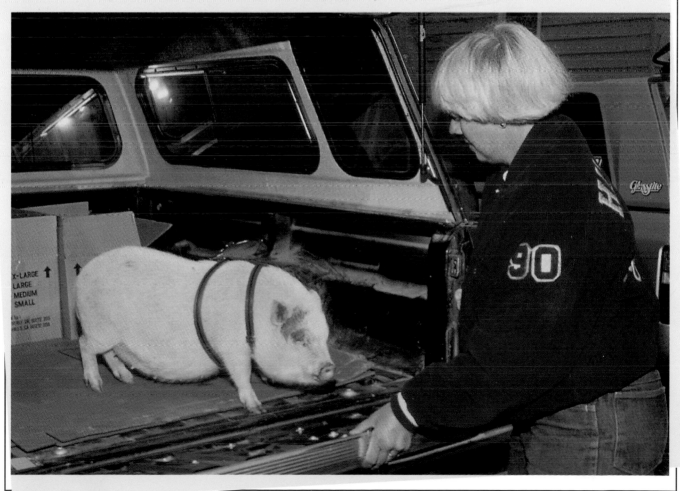

Some pigs enjoy travel more than do others. This piggy is a seasoned traveler and enjoys regular outings with members of her human family.

LIVING WITH PIGLET

You will view your piglet not so much as a porcine, but as a little mind that is waiting to be educated. You are aware that you too must learn—but in this instance, how to teach. Let us first look at what can happen when a piglet is not trained to live with humans as it should.

It will be unresponsive to its name. It may become very aggressive when forced to do something it does not want to do. It may attack any strangers who visit your home. It will foul your carpets and all other areas of your home just as it pleases. It may raid your food cupboards, and may even learn to open the refrigerator door and help itself. It will rip up clothes, chair covers and even your carpets. You will be unable to take it for a walk without regarding this as a battle. It will be reluctant to enter a crate if it needs to visit the vet—and when it gets there it may squeal so loudly all other patients will think the vet is killing it, rather than just commencing a routine examination. It may attack other small pets you own, or those of your neighbors if it gets half the chance.

Ultimately, it will reduce you to a nervous wreck, or you will be physically punishing it such that it is a neurotic, frightened and potentially dangerous animal. It will cease to be a pet and become a liability that will

have no chance of ever seeing its lifespan in your company. You will tire of it. All of this can and does happen for no other reason than the owner was either too lazy, too softhearted, or to heavy handed. More often than not this sort of owner will blame the breeder for selling them a

A pig that behaves well doesn't just happen...It has to be trained.

bad piglet, or they will blame the pig for being stupid. Rarely will they accept that they, and they alone, were totally responsible for being an incapable trainer and unsuitable owner.

If you are a first-time pig owner, and have never before owned and trained any other animal, be prepared to study books on training. Also, be prepared to accept that you, more than the pig, will need to learn, and that if problems arise, the cause of the problem is yourself. Training is all about communicating responses to your pet. If this cannot be done, the pet cannot be trained. If you

commence with this firmly in your mind, and are prepared to learn, you will make a good trainer. Your pet might still not be perfect, but it will be sufficiently trained that it becomes an integral and much loved member of your family.

BASIC NEEDS OF A TRAINED PIGLET

A pig is a highly intelligent mammal and is almost unlimited in what it can learn from a good trainer. However, all pet pigs should be trained to a minimum standard of behavior, and its accomplishments should include the following:

1. It should respond positively to its name.

2. It should be clean in its habits, meaning it should be litter box trained.

3. It should not be aggressive when touched, or when strangers enter your home.

4. It should not be destructive to your home.

5. It should walk nicely on a lead.

6. It should be quite willing to be transported about in a crate and a vehicle.

7. It should not become fearful and unsettled when in the midst of people, other pets and traffic.

8. It should not be a nuisance to you or any other person who is in your home.

None of these requirements are especially difficult for your pet to learn, but they do require a great deal of self control and determination on behalf of yourself, the trainer. Let us consider some basic ground rules that you must regard as sacrosanct with regards to teaching little porky.

TRAINING DO'S AND DON'TS

Do keep all lessons short—your piglet's powers of concentration have only a limited span. Remember, he is only a toddler. No more than five minutes should be devoted to training when your pet is young, but you can have more than one lesson over the course of a day.

Don't try to teach porky difficult tricks, or to do any task that would be physically difficult for a porcine. Your piglet is not a dog or a cat, and its physique must always be appreciated.

Do commence each lesson on an up note with a task your pet has already mastered. Give lots of praise for this which sets up the mood for the lesson to be learned.

Don't end a lesson on a down note. You must end with success and praise. If things haven't gone well, end with an easy task and give lots of praise. If things are going badly you should cease the lesson and play with your pet.

Do teach your pet only when you can obtain its full concentration. Initial training is best done when no one else is around, and when there are no distractions to compete for porky's concentration—such as other pets, children and especially food!

Don't rely too heavily on props, such as tidbits,

otherwise you will always need them.

Do, as your main training aid, fuss over and praise your piglet. Success is built on positives, not on negatives.

Don't use physical punishment when porky does not understand what you are trying to communicate to him or her. This merely insults your own intelligence. It means your lack of ability to communicate has reduced you to using violence because you cannot use your superior intelligence to devise another

Don't rely too heavily on food rewards when training your pot-belly. Praise and a gentle pat can be important too.

way to let your pet know what you want in respect of a response to an action or command. This does not mean the odd quick slap would not be inappropriate if the situation demands it.

It might seem that you must have to be almost an angel in order to train porky. As a beginner you will make many mistakes. All trainers

have at some point in their careers. It is their willingness to address errors that separates good trainers from bad ones. They learn just as their pupils do. You will find yourself getting frustrated, and you may start to snap at your pet. You may even slap porky for not doing what was expected.

This is a normal reality of life—that does not make it desirable, just a reality. Sometimes a beginner can read a book on training and when things do not go quite

they way the book states they begin to have doubts as to their own abilities, because of the things they have done. If you know you love your pet, and you know he or she must be trained for its own future welfare, and you can feel upset or annoyed at yourself for "giving in" to your temperament, you are making really good progress. You

Pot-bellies and kids can be great pals. Children can be taught to help care for the porcine member of the family.

little tidbits with you and start talking softly to porky. Let him or her walk around. Do not try to hold your pet at this time. Offer the treats and your pet will take them cautiously.

You must always try to let the youngster come to you—which it will out of curiosity. When you reach out to touch it, always let it see your hand (so keep this at its head level or lower). Move this very slowly towards the piglet so it can sniff it and become familiar with your scent. If you move, do this very slowly and while your pet is watching so it does not panic. Maybe you could read a book, or write some letters to pass the time away.

How long should you do this? This is difficult to state, but stay with your pet for as long as possible. Have the piglet's litter box in the room in case it wants to attend its needs. When the time is up gather your pet in your arms very carefully so as not to frighten it. Support its throat with one hand while placing the other around its flanks and under its chest, then bring it to your chest. In this position it will feel secure and less likely to struggle. Place it in its pen. Talk to it as often as possible. It might not understand your words, but it does understand the tone of your voice and associates this with affection, just as it did its mother who would talk to it with a series of muted grunts. Use its name often (and make the name short and simple so it will be more readily learned).

should determine yourself to be better and not let your feelings rule your mind. Success will come, and your pet will have no problems overlooking a few failings in your make-up. Never give up on your pet nor yourself, because you both lose from that situation.

BONDING—THE KEY TO SUCCESS

Before you can hope to have any real success at training an animal, you first need to create a growing bond between the both of you. Once your pet trusts you, and has confidence in you, it will want to please you. It will accept your discipline without developing any sort of fear "hang-ups." From the minute

you obtain your piglet every interaction you have with it will be shaping its thoughts of you. It will rapidly get to know what it can get away with and what it cannot. It will come to know what it can expect of you in respect to affection and attention.

Your first few days should be devoted to talking and generally playing with your pet. It needs to get used to the feel of your hands on its body. If it is already socialized, this will be very easy, but if it is not, you must go about this with great patience. Take your piglet to a bathroom or another small room. Sit yourself down as low to the ground as possible. This makes you less intimidating to a baby animal. Have some

COMING TO YOU

Probably the most important lesson you need to

teach your pet is to come to you when called. This must always be something porky associates with a nice ending—praise, petting, or some favored treat. Do not use treats all of the time. Eventually you want your pet to come to you for reasons of affection. As you move around your home call porky's name, bend down and praise him or her when they come. Do it often so that your pet will quickly learn its name and happily respond to it. Coming to you should never be associated with a negative response. You must always control your feelings in the event your pet has done something naughty some time earlier.

DISCIPLINE

All animals receive discipline in one form or another from their mother, father, or other older individuals of that species. It is essential for their future survival within a family unit or asocial group. Pigs are given a series of quick hard lessons about life as they grow up in the wild. They live in a hierarchical based society which is normally headed by a sow, and which has a number of juveniles at the bottom. When a youngster breaks a piggy "code" an older individual will quickly turn on it and bite or otherwise inflict pain on it to a greater or lesser degree. A pig has no problem accepting and coping with this situation: it learns from it.

Unfortunately, some well meaning but misguided pet owners often seem to overlook this fact when trying to train their pets. This is why you see neurotic and aggressive animals that cannot be trusted and will even snap at their owners and get away with it. Often, only their diminutive size prevents them from becoming really dangerous animals. So let us talk about discipline in a realistic manner.

Discipline is used on an animal in order to control its actions. It can be graded into many levels from merely the spoken word in a stern voice, through restraint on a harness and lead, to mild spanks and ultimately much more severe physical punishment. Physical punishment is the very last level that a trainer will resort to, and then only when the animal has become so aggressive that it is a positive danger to society such that unless retrained quickly it must be destroyed.

The level of discipline needed in order to train an animal to effect a given response is related to its age, its breeding, the way in which it is trained and the environment in which it lives. There should never be a need to inflict harsh physical punishment on any pet. Should this need ever arise it is because the owners were sentimental and lacking at an earlier time in the pet's life. Even then, it is possible to retrain an unresponsive pet without resorting to harsh punishment if sufficient time and care can be applied. In effect, a trainer would need to go right back to basics and start all over again.

As any trainer will tell you, praise and affection are easily the best tools you can have, but discipline is inevitable sooner or later. The minute

Some pot-bellied pigs enjoy the companionship of other family pets. Others do not. A lot depends on the personality of the individual pig.

you place restraint on a lead you are applying discipline. You are preventing the animal from doing what it wants to do. When you say "no" in a harsh voice this is discipline. It implies to the pet that if an action is not ceased, the level of "punishment" will rise. If the pet ignores the verbal

newspaper and, of course, your hand are further training tools.

What you must appreciate about discipline is that it is not so much what tool you choose to use as to when and how it is used. It must be at the very moment of a misdemeanor. Its level of

quite a number of months. It is no different to a small human baby in this respect. It will want to relieve itself after it wakes up from sleeping, after or during play, and a short while after it has eaten or had a drink. You should try to anticipate events based on this and place porky in its litter box at these times. Keep the box well away from food dishes as no animal likes to defecate near its own food place. Ideally, porky should be fed in a pen with the litter box placed at the opposite end to the food dish. When it has eaten it can rest and will normally use its box when it feels the urge.

It is always better to try and litter train a piglet in a confined space before it is allowed freedom to wander around your home. Otherwise, you will have no influence over where it chooses to attend its needs. It is even better if it has an outside pen or place to relieve itself. If this is so, it should be taken out frequently at the times mentioned and then lavishly praised when it does as required. You must be prepared to accept a number of mistakes when porky is small. Fortunately, the ammonia content of pig fecal matter is lower than that of dogs or cats, so it does not have quite the same bad odor.

If you see your pet fouling your carpet or other area, try to go over to it as quickly as possible, but without frightening it. Take it to its box and praise it. It probably will do nothing, but litter training has to be learned from praise rather than punishment. Once a spot has been fouled make sure it is

Good piggy! It is especially important to praise your pig when it first begins to use its litter box.

warning, you are then placed in the situation where you take matters to the next level, or you let the pet get away with whatever it is doing.

If you have a very young animal, you can apply discipline in its most mild form which is restraint or the tone of your voice. If training is neglected and the pet starts to develop bad habits, this will normally mean a somewhat harder level will be needed to convey to your pet what you will not accept of it. A very popular tool of discipline is a hand water spray, such as a child's water pistol. Others are a bunch of keys, or a tin can with pebbles in it. A roll of

intensity should be only that needed to effect an action, which will be to cease what porky is doing. The minute discipline has been administered, it must be an end to that matter. Further, if you can use a non-discipline method to achieve a given action, or to stop that which is undesirable, this is always preferred.

LITTER BOX TRAINING

Hopefully, you will have purchased a piglet that is already housetrained. If not, the following will help. First, your piglet has little control of its bowel movements, so do not expect it to have such for really well cleaned. Use one of the branded pet odor removers over the whole area. If it is possible, place an obstruction over the spot so your pet cannot use that place again. If porky is not being litter box trained in a confined area, it would be wise to have a number of boxes placed at strategic locations in a house or room. Constant surveillance and praise are the ways in which to toilet train your pig, and any other free roaming house pet.

If your pet starts to foul one particular room or location, it is important that this area is made out of bounds in one way or the other. If not, your pet's use of that place will become a habit. If things really start to get out of hand, do not punish porky but always remember the golden rule—"go back to basics." In other words, confine the pet to an area you can more easily monitor, and be ready to lavish praise for success. If your pet stands near to the outside door, never ignore him or her. Give praise and open the door. Go out with your pet and praise success. As your pet matures it will have more control over its bowels. If fed at regular times, you will come to know about what time it will need to relieve itself.

HARNESS TRAINING

The sooner your pet has become familiar with a harness the sooner you can start to train it to walk on a lead. A good breeder will have harness trained all piglets they sell. If this is not the case, the first thing to do is to establish a bond with the youngster so it has no problems in letting you touch its head, neck, throat, back and belly. Never attempt to fit the harness until the bonding is well established, otherwise you will badly frighten the piglet. It will associate the harness with fear and force.

Once the harness is on just let your pet carry on as normal. Some fussing over and a treat might seem

"Can we share it?" Piggy and pooch are on their best behavior.

appropriate so porky associates the harness with something nice happening. Do not fit a lead at this time. After a while you can remove the harness and give lots of fuss and a treat. Repeat this later in the day, and over the next day or two. Never leave the harness on for long periods once your pet is used to it. Fit it only when going out. This way your pet will come to associate the harness with going out, a pleasurable thing.

LEAD TRAINING

Once the harness is totally familiar to your porcine you can attach a lead to it. Keep this loose and let porky go where he or she wants. It is best to begin lead training in a quiet place, preferably where your pet's choice of directions is limited, such as a large garage or near a garden wall. Never commence lead training when there are distractions or things that might frighten your piglet. After a few minutes of walking you can take up the slack on the lead just enough that your pet can feel the restraint. The second porky reacts to the restraint let the lead slacken off again. Repeat this many times until your pet does not react like a bucking bronco at the state fair. You can encourage your piglet to go in your direction by enticing it with little treats.

After a few sessions you should be able to take porky around your garden and not have undue tantrums. A series of little tugs on the lead should be sufficient to encourage your pet to follow you. Once you have reached this stage you can now move onto the next, which is controlling porky to walk alongside of you. This is best done near a wall which restricts your pet's ability to move laterally (the wall one side and your leg the other). The lead is held in your right hand, which leaves your left hand free to tap your thigh. As porky starts to move ahead of your left leg you simply give a tug on the lead and say "heel." This is repeated until your pet slows down to walking pace. Keep the lessons short and praise porky when he or she is walking beside you. Some owners allow their pigs to walk ahead of them, but this is not a desirable position because it reduces the

because it will tend to place you off balance. With a small dog or piglet this would not happen, but with a stronger pet it can. Left handed owners will of course reverse these positions.

This is another lesson that should never involve other than a steady on/off restraint and a firm voice in the command. Patience and persistence are the keys to successful lead training—and of course regular practice. Once straight line walking is

porky, will need to prepare the piglet for both restriction in a crate and being transported in a vehicle. But even the housebound pet will need to be taken to the vet, so preparatory training is always beneficial.

A crate should be such that the piglet has ample head room, and is able to turn around if it so desires. As it matures, it will need a larger crate. You may decide to invest in a large one from the outset. It will make a good bed, so has more than one use. Use the crate to collect your pet from the breeder. Once at home, let porky go in and out of this as it pleases. A few tidbits at the far end will encourage use of the crate. Do not close your pet in this at first, wait until he has no problems in entering it.

The next stage is to close the door for short periods when porky is probably tired. The periods can be extended on a steady basis. Always provide your pet with a few food items when it is in the crate so it regards this as a nice place. Never force your porcine into a crate as this will simply make matters worse the next time.

Car training should also be done on a build up basis. Initially, you do not need to even leave your driveway. Place your pet in the car and sit with it. Give it a tidbit, thus reinforcing the notion that a car is a nice thing to be in. The first few excursions must be short and should always end by letting your pet out and having a nice walk. As always, your objective is to have your pet associate the car with a pleasurable experience. Occasionally there

Gradually introduce your pig to traveling by car. Start off with short trips. And don't forget the harness and lead.

effective control you have over your pet in the event of a problem. Likewise, a pig that trails behind you is also in a position that you have less control over.

The lead is held in the right hand. If your pet should bolt you are better able to hold on by bringing your left hand onto the lead. If you are holding the lead in the left hand, it is more difficult to bring the right hand into play

well understood, practice left turns, then right. Left turns are easier because your leg helps guide porky in the desired direction.

CRATE TRAINING & TRANSPORTATION

Crate training and transportation will be more important to some owners than to others. Those who take their pets on vacation with them, or plan to exhibit is the pet that never does take to car travel, in which case a sedative from your vet will make a long journey less disagreeable.

AVOIDING AGGRESSIVE TENDENCIES

Aggression in a pet rarely starts when it is an adult. Usually it develops in a juvenile. It is either encouraged by the owner, or is allowed to go unchecked in a toddler because it seems amusing and hardly dangerous. Never encourage a piglet to chase or charge someone by laughing, or in anyway giving the piglet reason to think that this action is desirable. What it does as a piglet it will do with more deadly intent as an adult, and will be much more difficult to correct without resorting to physical punishment.

Sometimes aggression comes about because the pet feels insecure, which means you are doing something wrong. Maybe you are inconsistent in the way you are treating your pet. Maybe you or another family member are teasing the pet, which is the quickest way to make a pet unreliable. It may also be that your pet does not see many strangers and is thus very defensive when it does. This is easily avoided introducing porky to as many people as possible when he or she is tiny. Let them fuss over your pet and touch it.

If your pet starts to use its mouth to grasp your hand and bites too hard, you should quickly pull your hand away and say "no" in a firm voice. Alternatively, clench your fingers and push (not punch) these into porky's mouth so he or she realizes that what it bites can also create discomfort. It must learn to discriminate in how it uses its mouth. If your pet should ever give you a hard nip give it a rapid tap on its snout, hard enough to be uncomfortable, but not so hard that it would really hurt. At the same time say "no" very firmly. It is the surprise of your reaction, coupled with the verbal admonishment, that usually gets the message to your pet. But remember, your action in response to your pet's must be instant if it is to be effective and fully related to porky's action. This is most important with any form of firmer discipline. If you act promptly to any signs of aggression, they will be stopped before they get worse. It is no action or overreaction that creates a dangerous pet.

USING DISCIPLINARY AIDS

It does not always happen that your pet commits a misdemeanor when you are close enough to stop the action promptly. Sometimes acts are committed when you are not present at all, such as tearing up clothes or raiding the pantry. To overcome these situations the water pistol, a bunch of keys or pebble filled tin can will be useful disciplinary aids. If porky is doing something naughty while you are there, but at a distance, squirt him or her with the water, or throw the bunch of keys at the hindquarters (never the head in case of injury). The benefit of this action is that your pet does not associate the sudden arrival of water or keys with you! It is as though the action porky is doing has created them.

If your pet is prone to raid the pantry when you are out, the answer is to either confine your pet to a safe place, or to hide discreetly and wait for the culprit to strike! Then you blast the water or throw the tin can. Again, it is the total element of surprise that is hoped to fix in the pet's mind the notion that raiding the pantry always results in a negative conclusion. However, sometimes the desire to eat may override temporary discomfort and a new approach will then be needed. In this instance it will be confinement, or ensuring the pet cannot get into the pantry.

AFTER THE BASICS ARE LEARNED

Once you have trained your piglet in the basics of living with humans, you should not stop the training. This will leave a void in your pet's mental activity. You can progress to more advanced lessons, such as the "sit" and "down" commands. You can also teach your pet simple tricks. This constant interaction with porky will ensure your porcine remains a placid, very well balanced and loving pet. It keeps him or her from becoming bored.

If ever you find that your pet is regressing in any way, always return to basic training as a refresher course. Never let training become a mindless exercise. The best way to overcome this is to take your pet on outings to different places and effect the training. Completing its lessons under a growing range of conditions will make for a more educated and experienced pet.

BREEDING THEORY

When a person or couple decide to become breeders, in any species, they do not always give a great deal of thought to breeding theory. This is unfortunate because it immediately restricts their potential progress. A good boar and sow will be needed, and many will assume that if the initial stock is from a winning breeder, it must be good, and that if they pay a given sum, this is what they will get. This is not necessarily so. If mating a sow to a top boar, many will think that the quality of the offspring should be good; this may not be so.

The fact that a breeding book was written for a dog, horse, budgerigar or cattle breeder does not change the theory of the subject as applied to your pets. Once basic principles are understood it becomes a case of trying to find out what genetic facts are known about pigs in general, and pot-bellied in particular, and then applying these to the principles learned. Before we look at some aspects of theory, we will consider practical requirements of a breeding program.

BREEDING RECORDS

The very first thing you must determine you will do as a breeder is to keep detailed breeding records. Without these you cannot realistically apply good breeding theory. Breeding records overcome the innate problems of using your memory to determine the value of past pigs.

A breeding record can be as simple or as detailed as you wish to make it. Its great value is that it documents realities. From these you may be able to trace problems, and virtues, through the many individuals you breed over the years. It should contain the following basic data:

Each individual you retain for breeding will have their own record card. This will indicate their sire and dam. It will document the registration number, color pattern (including genotype if any part of this is known for sure), ID number of the individual, its sex, size (measured accurately), adult weight, how many times bred, how many offspring were born, and how many survived to selling age. It should indicate what illnesses were contracted and what problems were encountered, if any, during breeding. It will eventually give the age at death and the cause of this, be it a disease, accident, or natural (old age).

The record may include a photo of the pig, or at the least a sketch of its pattern if this is other than a solid color. It can also contain details of major show success, or of offspring that have achieved fame of one sort or another. If a genetic defect becomes apparent, or is known to have been recognized in any of its offspring, this must be documented. If you ignore any facts because you do not like them, or because they might devalue a given individual if they became known, you are then doing a great disservice to yourself, which will catch up with you at a later date, and the hobby as a whole. Sadly, this situation is not uncommon in any pet hobby that becomes popular and involves either or both money and fame.

The breeding card itself will detail the sire and dam, and their registration numbers. It might include brief details of the boar if this was not owned by you (size, weight, age at mating, color, owner etc). It will indicate when a mating took place and whether this was a natural one or artificial insemination. It will document the farrowing date, number of piglets, their colors and weights at given times. Details of the diets given and date of vaccinations would be useful data, as will notes on any problems or illnesses experienced between birth and selling. Deformities must of course be documented. It will indicate when piglets were desexed and to whom stock was sold. The cards become a total history of all of your breeding program, and will become an essential aid in many ways.

PEDIGREES

There are a lot of

misconceptions held about pedigrees, and these persist with many breeders, not just with pet owners. A pedigree is a written indicator of a line of descent. In the absence of your having knowledge of the individuals on the pedigree, it is nothing more than a scrap of paper. The fact that it displays a host of champions it could be, in a nutshell, a load of rubbish.

The fact that a given illustrious champion was a sire is often used to hike up the price of all the piglets, but, a piglet's worth is no more than what you see in front of you. If it is mediocre, its price and pedigree is worth just that. Any higher value will be aspects and the real value of the pig based on its quality.

The fact that a pig may have been the result of inbreeding is sometimes regarded as a negative. Some breeders will boast that their pigs are excellent because they are carefully line bred. Again, these are merely terms (and a lot more variable than

Breeding pot-bellies—or any other pet—is a matter that deserves serious consideration. If you don't have the considerable time and resources that are necessary to maintain a breeding program, don't breed your pig.

and top winners means nothing of itself, but people tend to be dazzled by these. They assume it indicates their pig is something special, when based on other factors, such as how well it has been cared for, if it has been socialized and so on. You must distinguish between these is generally realized), which some breeders do not actually understand anyway, even though they use them. All pot-bellied pigs in the USA,

Canada, and other Western countries are inbred, it being a case of to what degree. This is obvious when you stop to consider they were all derived from such a small nucleus of imports only a few years ago. The fact that you look on a pedigree and see that a given pig was the result of a sibling or half sibling mating does not mean it is an inferior animal or represented poor breeding. You would need to know a lot more about the individuals to be able to make such an assessment. Herein lies the only way in which you can draw conclusions from a pedigree. You must have an intimate knowledge of the individuals on it. Without this it is quite impossible to say whether it is good or bad.

A piglet may have no champions in its pedigree yet it could be far superior to one studded with these, and be a much better potential breeding pig. The most important generations in a pedigree are those close to that of your piglet; beyond the third, the influence of the ancestors starts to recede dramatically. What you should therefore do when reading a pedigree is to find out as much as you can about the grandparents and their parents. This will be much more valuable to you than dwelling too long on some famous ancestor four or five generations back.

Inexperienced breeders (and these may include some people who have been in a hobby for years) devote far to much attention to the "big" names in a pedigree. They seem to forget that those unknown sows contributed every bit as much to the onward generations as their more famous boars. It is obviously beneficial to know about the famous boars, but this is only part of the picture. You must know what the quality of the sows was, as well as other boars in the pedigree, in order to more accurately assess the likely genotype of your own pigs for the features you are selecting for. Without such a knowledge you purchase stock, and plan matings, at your peril.

There are two aspects often

This male (the white pig) is about to mount the female. When selecting pot-bellies for breeding, start with animals of high quality. The results will be well worth it.

overlooked. The first is that a given stud may be owned by someone who has no shortage of cash available to promote the boar via exhibitions and advertising. This results in the boar's name becoming familiar to potential users, and results in greater use. The owner can then promote facts such as "the most widely used boar" and similar statements which may be quite true. To the novice the assumption is that the boar must be good.

The average breeder is unaware how many times a boar has been mated, how many offspring it has sired, of those offspring how many were regarded as being of no merit at all, or displayed a serious defect, poor color, or other feature that is held to be of importance in a pet such as the pot-bellied. This all means that the only realistic way you can assess the worth of a given breeding animal is via the overall standard of the offspring it has produced. In a pet species where there is no accurate measurable yardstick of quality, show ring success becomes this.

Using this as the measure of quality or breeding value, you would need to find out the percentage of winning stock a boar had produced compared to the total number of offspring sired. This figure would be your best guide to its worth because it enables you to make at least some sort of comparison that nullifies the fact it had greater opportunity to be used. If it is a very well known boar you must also bear in mind the fact that it will also have had a greater opportunity to cover the best sows around.

If its performance in terms of winning progeny was not especially impressive, when

course, it may happen that the best boar in the hobby is the most promoted. The only way you can find out is by a lot of diligent work. The reality is that many breeders will not devote the needed time to this.

The second aspect on this subject is that many breeders have little or no understanding of how characteristics are passed from one generation to the next. Two very similar looking boars of outstanding merit may be totally different in

offspring 50% of its genes, never more, nor less, as is sometimes bandied about in animal hobbies. If a pig looks more like one parent than another this is not because it received more genes from that parent, but for other reasons that space does not permit discussion of.

Now, with this basic information let us consider our two outstanding pigs, but in respect of their possible genotypes. Pig A has a genotype of **AABBCCDDEEFF** while pig B has **AaBbCcDdEeFf**. If we assume that **ABCDEF** are dominant genes for the desired visual appearance (phenotype), it can be seen that the B pig will indeed look as good as pig A. All of its negative genes are in single recessive form, so are not seen visually.

Mating. The gestation period in pot-bellied pigs ranges from 106 to 116 days.

compared to lesser known boars, and given its tremendous starting advantages, you can assume it is at best an overrated individual. At worst, it is no better than hundreds of others boars in the population, any of which may have been less costly to use and may have passed on more virtues and less faults. Of

their ability to pass their merit to future generations.

For those admitting to no genetic knowledge, features are passed to each subsequent generation by genes. For each feature there will be at least one pair of these genes. Of these, one gene will have been received from each of the parents. Each parent thus gives its

When it comes to breeding time, pig A can only pass on the genes **ABCDEF** because it is pure (homozygous) for these at each loci(the site of a given pair of genes on a chromosome). As a result, its offspring are guaranteed inheriting, from that parent, only desirable genes for the features covered. Now consider pig B. Its offspring may indeed inherit only **ABCDEF**. But, and the chances are equally as good, they (or some of them) could inherit **abcdef**, which are totally unwanted genes— hardly what was expected from such an outstanding male. In reality, most of the offspring will inherit some of each. For example, they may be **ABcDe**, or other comparable combinations. They will receive some dominant desirables, but some undesirables.

In the example I have suggested that the desirable features are always controlled by dominants, which may not be the case in reality. However, what is more true to state is that most unwanted features (from an evolutionary standpoint) are carried as recessives.

Now we must consider the second parent. Let us assume the sow has the genotype of **AaBBccDdeeFF**. She is a nice female but rather weak in the features controlled by the genes **c** and **e**. She is also weak (but unbeknown to her owner) from a breeding point in features **a** and **d**. The boar was chosen because he looked very good in all the features. Taking a worst case scenario the offspring might inherit **aBcdeF** from the sow. From the boar they could receive **abcdef**, so will have a genotype of **aaBbccddeeFf**.

Feature **A**, which looked fine in both parents, has regressed to be terrible in the offspring carrying that genotype. This could not have happened had boar A been used. At the worst the offspring would have been no different to their mother in looks and genotype.

Feature **B** has degenerated from **BB** in the mother to **Bb** in the offspring. The feature still looks good, but was pure good in the mother, now it contains an unwanted recessive **b** that will no doubt turn up in later generations. That could not have happened with pig A. Feature **C**, which was a noticeable fault in the mother, is still a noticeable fault in the offspring. It is possible that if the boar had passed its **C** gene the feature would have improved. However, note the word "possible." Had pig A been used you could say the feature

is "guaranteed" to look good.

Moving to features **DEF** the same scenario of "could be worse" in the offspring is the reality, which could not happen had pig A been used. The owner of the sow would be extremely disappointed if he or she had used pig B because it was so highly thought of in the show ring. The point that this example really underscores is the fact that the route by which two given super boars gain their looks may be totally different from a genetic standpoint. This does not devalue their worth as show winners, they are still gorgeous pigs. It is a case that pig A can pass "gorgeous" with almost certainty to its offspring, pig B would need a mathematical miracle to pass all its good features on. Such has happened, but it is akin to winning a lottery, and begs the question "would you like to gamble on those sort of odds in your breeding program?" That's exactly what you will be doing if you use a boar simply because it is a big winner, after having read this text. Do not blame the boar, or its owner, if the results disappoint you!

THE VALUE OF THE SOW

With all this talk of boars, let us not forget just how important the female of the species is in the way of things. You do not need to own a boar—ever—to be a breeder, but you will need one or more sows! Her quality is of paramount importance to you because she will probably be the founding mother to all of your future stock. You can use any number of boars over a number of years, but your herd will probably develop

When a sow is pregnant, her belly may hang to the ground even lower than usual.

from just one or two females and their offspring. On their faults and virtues will rest the total success and failure of your program. Actually, we must add another factor, which is your own ability to select good onward stock from that produced.

THE CONSEQUENCE OF INBREEDING

Earlier, I implied that inbreeding per se was not detrimental to a breeding program. Indeed, it is almost obligatory when a new animal hobby starts up. Most faults in an animal are carried in recessive (unseen) form. By inbreeding you dramatically increase the chances that these recessives will come together and manifest themselves, when you can then begin the process of trying to eliminate them. Likewise, visible virtues can be fixed into the individual, or population (be this your herd or the population as a whole). A recessive fault may be related to an eye disease, to an ear problem, and so on. Inbreeding can ultimately remove these from a population, thus it has obvious benefits in the hands of a skillful and knowledgeable breeder. On the negative side, in the process of inbreeding a very high proportion of undesirable offspring may be produced and need to be culled.

If a pair of pigs have no given undesirable fault in their genotype, then no amount of inbreeding will introduce that fault. As a result, many top winning dogs, cats, rabbits, budgerigars and pigs, to name but a few, are the result of

This black and white sow is pregnant. Obesity in pigs should be prevented, especially in pregnant females.

inbreeding to a greater or lesser degree; the lesser is called linebreeding. Once close inbreeding has been practiced for one or two generations, there is really no advantage in continuing with it because other negatives may then start to come into play. This point is extremely important in pigs. Those who persistently inbreed in order to reduce the size, or improve appearance, of these pets are clearly blatantly unaware of this.

All studies in breeding populations have clearly shown that all organisms resist extreme change from that evolved as being normal. There is also a need for a population to retain a reasonable level of heterozygosity if full vigor is to be maintained. What uninformed inbreeders do not seem aware of is that many features in an animal are not

visual. For example, traits such as intelligence, docility, breeding vigor, longevity, ability to resist disease, milk production in the female, birth weight of infants, survival expectations of embryos, mothering instincts, and many other aspects can only be assessed over a number of generations.

SELECTION AND GRADING OF YOUNG STOCK

It matters not how outstanding your breeding stock is if you are incapable of making sound judgments in respect of evaluating the offspring you will retain for future breeding. A good breeder can start with only mediocre stock and over a period of years steadily upgrade this by judicious selections. A poor breeder can have access to the best stock in the world and steadily

The farrowing, or birthing, pen can be equipped with a heat lamp so that the newly born piglets can be kept safely warm.

downgrade this if they cannot make good progeny selections.

The way in which you decide to grade offspring from given matings will be as important to you as was the choice of your breeding stock in the first place. Before you can attempt to grade you must determine what the objectives are for the grading. For example, you may wish to concentrate on improving one, at most two, features at a time (known as tandem selection). Alternatively, you may feel that your preferred strategy is to raise the overall standard of your stock at each generation (independent culling or total score selection). If you adopt the former method you can obtain results faster than in the latter.

On the negative side, when you move on to another feature the original feature that was upgraded may be adversely affected. If you use a total upgrade strategy, you will see some positive movement of a feature and

some regression in others, but the overall situation will hopefully be to the good. The problem is that this can be a long term policy and many breeders do not have the patience to wait that long. Whatever your objectives are, you should stick with them for long enough to decide if you are making progress. A temptation is to be continually swapping objectives at each generation; this is rarely successful.

Having decided on your objectives you need to be able to grade the stock for these in some way that is both effective and consistent. Again, many breeders do get carried away by a feature that is seen in a youngster that is not, in the fullness of their program, that important. As a result they may retain a given individual without realizing that it may not really have been the best choice to retain.

If you decide to upgrade across a number of features, you may do this in one of two

ways. You can give each feature a set number of points then select offspring who meet the minimum requirements for **every** feature. If an individual excels in one or two features, but is rather below the minimums decided upon, then it will not be used. You are concerned only with those individuals that meet a given standard on all features. Of course, you must be capable of making consistent judgments at each litter otherwise any grading system will have little value unless it is based on exact measurements, as in milk production, fat thickness, and other features that the average pet breeder is not concerned with.

A variation on general upgrading would be to give each feature a number of points, say 10, and then place these in their order of importance to you. Each is then given a coefficient number. For example, if shoulder height was your prime objective this might have a coefficient of 5, head structure might be given 4, while color might have 3. Backlength may be good in your stock so would carry only 2. Each feature is then scored out of ten and multiplied by its coefficient to produce a total score. You then retain for breeding those with a predetermined total minimum.

What this method does is to remove any possibility that you might be tempted to retain a piglet because it excelled in a feature that was not so important. That feature would have only a low coefficient. Even if it outscored shoulder height out of ten, its total score would still probably be lower, thus retaining the emphasis on shoulder height.

With any such system you must determine the coefficient with great care lest it be unbalanced and does not serve its purpose. You must also be sure that the features given high coefficients are really that bad or good as the case may be. Only an expert could advise you on these. Once the most needed feature is upgraded you then lower its coefficient and raise that of other improvements needed. However, you may decide that once improved you wish to maintain the standard of the feature, in which case it might always have a high coefficient number.

Health and breeding vigor should always have high values, indeed they are the most important features, so should arguably be the highest two coefficients, ahead of temperament. This should ensure that your stock only improves in its type if these three key traits are maintained as the major priorities.

You might also remember that a piglet does change as it gets older, so it would be wise to grade your stock at a range of ages and see how the gradings then look. In Japanese colored carp (koi) this is exactly how the very best fish are selected, but it does mean you must have the facility and cash to afford the luxury of running stock beyond the age when most breeders would sell them. But it does maximize the potential of your breeding. In grading your stock you are also affecting what is known as progeny testing. Based on the results of this you can set

A sow inspecting her farrowing pen. The interior of a farrowing pen is specially designed to help prevent a sow from crushing her babies when she lies down.

values on the breeding worth of the parents. By pairing a sow with different boars, then grading their offspring, you are able to decide which adults are best used as the driving force of your program. When an experienced breeder sees many pigs at a show, and inquires as to the sire and dam of those that are most impressive, they are actually conducting a form of progeny testing. When they are satisfied as to the worth of a given male they will use it. In the case of a sow, they may try to buy her.

Litter size in pot-bellied pigs can range from 1 to 12, but typically is around 4 to 8.

THE STANDARD AND COLORS

A standard of excellence is a blueprint of what is deemed desirable. It is an extremely important document to any relatively new pet because it lays down the criteria breeders will initially use in determining their breeding

A pot-belly that is not of show quality can make as good a pet as can an exhibition pot-belly.

strategy and programs. Breeding programs will later be influenced by how others interpret the standard. If it is vague, it will be interpreted in an array of ways that will not be conducive to the best interests of the hobby. If it is too precise, it will be almost impossible for breeders to

produce a pot-belly that reasonably conforms to it.

The standard must be weighted carefully so that it does not place too much emphasis (points) on a given feature such that this results in overexaggeration of that feature. But it should reflect those aspects of the breed that are held to be of the utmost importance.

Although a standard, by stating what is required, clearly implies that anything other than this is undesirable, it should nonetheless draw attention to particular faults

that are likely to be subject to deterioration unless special care is exercised. Further, it should also, by way of automatic disqualification or withholding of high honors, make it quite clear what is absolutely unacceptable and what is very undesirable. This allows no room for interpretation, thus downgrading what can otherwise become a negative trend. This has the advantage that known genetic and other major faults will be actively outlawed, or at the least heavily penalized. They will not, as a consequence, be so readily spread through the breed.

The standard is thus not an easy document to draft. It is made all the more difficult in a pet like the pot-belly where quality is based on features that are esthetic and subjective rather than easily definable and measurable. It must never be unchangeable if it is to be realistic. It should always reflect the needs of the pot-belly, but never be adjusted to accommodate what has happened in the breed merely so that it fits the majority of exhibits if changes that have taken place are not deemed in the best interests of the pig itself. Unfortunately, a study of many popular pets will clearly show that "in the best interest of the animal" is often not a matter given much consideration in certain breeds.

This of course all means that those who draft a standard must have an in depth knowledge of the breed, of the genetic consequences of failing to address important issues before, rather than after an event, and have the strength of conviction to act when a negative trend or fashion is clearly perceived.

The standard can only ever be as meaningful as those who interpret it, which effectively means the judges. Although it is not a desirable state, the fact is most breeders react to judges rather than breed to the standard. If they are guilty of misinterpreting the standard, it is invariably because judges have allowed this to happen in the first place. The standard itself can leave too much room for individual interpretation, and breeders will fail to study and really try to understand what the standard is all about.

With these introductory comments setting the scene, the standard of the NCOPP is quoted, and comments on it are made in order to provide food for thought for the first time exhibitor or breeder. I have chosen to quote only the NCOPP standard because it is more detailed than that of NAPPA, allocates points to features, and includes color descriptions. The NAPPA standard is otherwise basically similar, except in placing a maximum height of 18in. on this breed. The comments made are equally applicable to it.

NCOPP SCORECARD 1993
Reproduced by kind permission of the National Committees On Pot-bellied Pigs.

A. General Appearance, 10 Points
A harmonious blending of all parts of the pig and how these parts fit together to produce an impressive style and carriage including conditioning, breed characteristics and show presence in the show ring. Conditioning includes healthy skin, hair and proper body weight.

B. Disposition, 15 Points
Disposition to be calm, friendly and tractable in the

The sway of the back should be moderate in proportion to the length of the pig. A sway that is overly exaggerated is undesirable.

ring. Biting, squealing, ill-behaved pigs will be excused from the ring by the judge. Piglets will show more nervousness than adults and may be allowed more leeway, but not to the extent that they upset the rest of the class.

C. Head, 15 Points
Includes: Face, nose, ears, jowl, eyes, bite

1. Face—Medium to wide in proportion to the rest of the head (a long, narrow face is undesirable).

2. Nose—Short to medium in length, allowing for free passage of air without wheezing when at rest.

3. Ears—Small, erect, somewhat flat.

4. Jowl—Obvious jowl, medium to full and in proportion to head.

5. Eyes—Deep, wide set, clear (bug eyes are undesirable).

6. Bite—Bottom teeth naturally protrude beyond top teeth to accommodate the scooping action while eating or rooting. Short nosed pigs will show this to a greater

A pig uses its nose for rooting and foraging. In a good specimen, the nose will be short to medium in length.

degree than medium nosed pigs. (Severe cases of overshot or undershot are severe defects.)

D. Front Body, 15 Points

Includes: Neck, chest, shoulders

1. Neck—Reasonably short, solid, blending smoothly into shoulders and jowl.

2. Top of shoulder—Level and smooth tying into shoulder.

3. Chest—Wide, deep, good heart girth (heart girth determines depth of chest).

4. Shoulders—Well-developed, muscular, but without exaggeration.

E. Body, 15 Points

Includes: Belly, back, height

1. Back—Moderate sway of back in proportion to the length of the pig. A short back, or "cobby" pig, is

desirable and will show less sway to the back than a long-bodied pig. Length of body must be considered when evaluating sway. (An overly exaggerated sway is undesirable.)

2. Belly—When viewed from the side, the pig should show an obviously rounded belly but not so exaggerated as to touch or drag on the ground. When viewed from the top down, there should only be a slight protuberance where back and side flow into the belly. Pregnant females are the exception to the rule.

3. Height—Maximum acceptable height at any age is 21 inches at the top of the shoulder.

Note: When scoring size, the intentional stunting of pigs by lack of proper food is inhumane and counter

productive to the good of the pot-bellied industry. Any such practice is to be severely penalized and such a pig will be ineligible for an award in the ring regardless of the number of pigs entered in that class.

Signs of Stunting: Coarse, rough haircoat, usually standing out from the body. A general debilitated state or unthriftiness. Hind legs carried close together, or touching, due to lack of muscle mass and fat in the rump area. A hunkered stance with hind legs well up under the pig, showing a pronounced bow of the back.

F. Back Body, 15 Points

Includes: Rump, hips, vulva, teats, testicles, tail

1. Rump—Full and level, flowing gently to the base of the tail. (Rounded or angular rump with a low hung tail is undesirable.)

2. Hips or Hams—Well-muscled and firm. When viewed from the rear, should blend into the rump with a gentle roundness.

3. Vulva—Of adequate size and placement.

4. Teats—At least five evenly spaced teats on each side. Inverted teats are penalized. Placement and number of teats are important in boars.

5. Testicles—Boars must have two visible testicles of proper size and development for their age.

6. Tail—Straight, attaches high on the rump.

G. Legs and Movement, 15 Points

Includes: Legs, forelegs, hind legs, feet, movement

1. Legs—Strong-boned, short pasterns, sound.

2. Forelegs—Good width

between, nearly straight to the knee, standing well on the pasterns.

3. Hind legs—Good width between legs when viewed from the rear. Hocks being nearly straight or only slightly turned in (hocks too close together or touching is undesirable). Perpendicular from hock to pastern from side view.

4. Feet—Two toes pointing forward, being nearly equal in length, showing normal placement and size of dewclaws.

5. Movement—A smooth flowing motion, free of limps or irregular, constricted movement. Front and rear legs should move out freely.

TOTAL 100 Points

Note: As long as the animal conforms to breed standards, color and/or markings shall in no way be a factor in determining placement in conformation classes.

COLOR STANDARDS

These standards are strictly color definitions whose purpose is to be descriptive. They are not to suggest or imply one color or pattern is better than another.

Black: Solid black with no other markings of any other sort on any part of the body including the leather or the snout.

Black/White Markings: Any white markings on black which include, but not

The ears should be small, erect, and somewhat flat. Note how the hair is thinned out on the sides of the face.

limited to, socks, stockings, stars, blazes, white tip tail, white tuft on the head, snout markings, white belly and white collar (partial, half or full).

Collar Pig: Must have a full collar which does not connect to the belly.

Pinto: The ground color of the body should be white with a "black saddle" which does not intermingle with itself except at the back legs. The black saddle may include the head of the pig and extend the length of the body or less. Other black markings are acceptable as in a black spot on belly, black head etc. The face can include white markings which include, but are not limited to, stars, blazes, white tufts on the head, etc. The pinto may or may not have a white collar.

Fancy Pinto: Same as pinto. However, the saddle has a halo. A halo is where the hair overlaps the skin color. For example, white hair laying over black skin. The saddle does not intermingle with itself and the saddle edges must be seen from the side and rear view of the pig.

Smooth Saddled Fancy Pinto: Same as fancy pinto. However, the halo width of the saddle is consistent around the edges of the saddle.

White: Solid white hair with pink skin and no other markings of any sort on any part of the body including a pink leather snout.

White/Black Markings: Any black patch skin pigment markings on white including, but not limited to, behind the ears, snout markings, on the head, jowls, throat, withers, rump, etc.

The forelegs should have good width in between, nearly straight to the knee.

Pebble: Solid white pig with gray, silver, or black "pebble spots" located, but not limited to, behind ears on the head, jowls, throat, withers or entire body.

Silver: Solid silver pig with no other markings. Color can vary from champagne silver, gray silver, blue silver, ash silver, etc.

Silver Pinto: The ground color of the body should be ivory with a "silver saddle" which does not intermingle with itself except at the back legs. The silver saddle may include the head of the pig and extend the length of the body or less. Other silver markings are acceptable as in a silver spot on the belly, silver head, etc. The face can

include ivory markings which include, but are not limited to, stars, blazes, white tufts on the head, snout markings, etc.

Fancy Silver Pinto: Same as silver pinto. However, the saddle has a halo. The saddle does not intermingle with itself, and the saddle edges must be seen from the sided and rear view of the pig.

Any Other Variety: Includes any other color variety.

Eye color is not a factor in determining color descriptions.

The tops of the shoulders should be level and smooth tying into the chest. The chest should be wide, deep, and with good heart girth.

COMMENTS ON THE STANDARD

Compared to the previous standard, the 1993 version shows a number of changes which should prove to be beneficial. Disposition is given a greater value, while the bite is explained rather better. The allocation of 10 points for General Appearance is a very positive move. It should give judges greater leeway to credit an exhibit for its overall quality, even if it has some faults on a feature by feature basis that might otherwise have denied it the opportunity to compete for the coveted blue ribbon, or even a placing.

The raised height maximum of 21 inches compared to the previous 18 inches might seem to some breeders a strange change at a time when many breeders are determined to boast of ever smaller pigs. However, it reflects the reality of producing good pot-bellied pigs, rather than those which are small but possibly lacking in quality. There is also the matter of zoning to consider with these pets. This would not normally be a consideration in other pet hobbies. If a low maximum height is stipulated and this is accepted by local councils, then a pig exceeding this might be classified as a farm pig. It would therefore seem prudent to maintain a realistic height even if the long term target is for smaller stock.

In the 1992 standard there was a total of 11 features that were allocated points and this has been reduced to 7 in the present standard. This I feel is sound judgment, though not everyone would agree with this comment. The pot-belly is very much in its infancy, both as a pet and from the development of the standard viewpoint. The more features that are given specific points early on in the hobby development, the greater the pressure on the judges to be very consistent in their markings of these. Further, it assumes that the allocation of the points to given features has been sound. It takes time for a judge to become really intimate with these pets from a judging perspective. The more features they have to score, the greater the risk that inconsistencies will arise, not because the judges are necessarily incompetent (though this may be so in some instances) but simply because experience does not come overnight.

Presently, the standard calls for a short to medium nose (snout) which is fine, as is the reference to the need for allowing free passage of air. However, a characteristic in this breed are facial wrinkles, which are not mentioned at all in the standard. Given that breeders are producing ever smaller pot-bellies, it is probable that excessive wrinkles and button nose or Peke-faces will become a matter of some concern. When this happens, the accompanying problems will be in relation to more sunken eyes, breathing difficulties, faulty dentition and greater facial susceptibility to parasitic invasion. Unless breeders have guidelines in the standard with respect to excessive facial skin folds, the observations drawn from

other pets strongly suggests that these will be regarded as more desirable in a pig than an individual with more moderate wrinkles, so very short snouted pigs will result.

The only realistic way to gain a meaningful concept of what actually is a desirable length is if this is related to shoulder height. This enables a definable ratio to be established and which would be applicable to any size of

Facial wrinkles are another characteristic of pot-bellied pigs.

pig. If care is not taken, there will be an ever growing incidence of pregnant sows having to be given belly supports to avoid their underparts dragging the ground. This is surely not conducive to the object of ensuring the standard protects this breed from the physical problems that will be a direct consequence of overlong backs and/or short legs.

The pot-bellied pig is rather unique among pets in that NAPPA and NCOPP, when drafting their standards, have very little leeway for error in numerous areas of potential exaggeration. Those who prepared the blue prints for dogs, cats, rabbits, horses and other pets did so against a background where anatomical deviations away from the wild type were not excessive. That negative genetic abnormalities were later allowed to become the basis for breeds, is to the discredit of the associations that sponsor and actively promote them.

Red eye, and where black in the coat is reduced to sepia, sandy, and recessive white, are examples of colors that are under breeder control in pig breeds, along with those already mentioned. However, a given color/

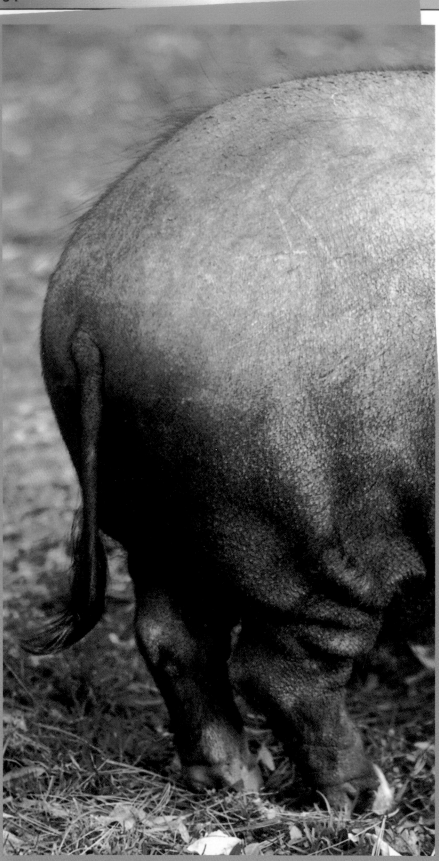

The pot-belly's tail is straight and is attached high on the rump.

pattern may have two totally differing genotypes with the same breed, where genes controlling color are not always at the same gene loci. Therefore, two individuals with the same color pattern could be paired and their offspring may display quite a different color or pattern. What is needed in the pot-bellied pig is a careful study of color breeding records so that geneticists can steadily develop a gene map that will help determine the likely means of color transmission in this breed.

The standard is not merely a description of the breed, but a document that has far reaching effects in how the pot-bellied pig will be developed in the coming years. If you become a breeder and/or exhibitor, you are strongly advised to read your standard on a regular basis. The objective of this is not simply to learn it parrot fashion, but to think carefully on what it means and how it should be interpreted. This can only come after long discussions with more knowledgeable enthusiasts, breeders and judges.

It is *your* standard and will affect your individual situation, so always take a keen interest in it. Do not be afraid to comment on it to your association. It is by the collective input from all involved with pot-bellied pigs that standards should steadily improve to the benefit of both the pigs and those who care for them—the hobbyists.

Like many aspects of animal husbandry, the main need to ensure your little piglet remains in good health is no more than the application of sound common sense. Armed with a good measure of this, and the ability to observe abnormal behavior and obvious clinical signs of ill health, you can stop, or at the least reduce the effect of, an illness should it arise. If you wish to study any aspect of animal health management, do not unduly waste your time studying treatments of specific diseases. Concentrate on preventative husbandry techniques related to those diseases. This means have a good knowledge of pathogenic control.

With such knowledge you will minimize any disease from ever being a problem. As a bonus you will be well positioned to prevent illness in any other pet.

THE CAUSE OF DISEASE AND HEALTH PROBLEMS

Clearly, diseases are caused by organisms that are parasitic upon their host. However, it is not so much that these organisms are on the host, but the fact that they are able to multiply. Many pathogens continually exist on and in a host, such as your pig, and they are all around your home in the atmosphere just waiting for an opportunity to multiply in large numbers.

When given the opportunity to multiply, that is the cause of a disease.

If you can prevent harmful bacteria from multiplying, you can keep their numbers down to a level where they are unable to overwhelm the natural defense mechanisms of your pet. At the same time

Contrary to popular belief, pigs are not dirty animals. Clean your piggie's outdoor enclosure on a regular basis.

you must be able to maintain these natural defenses by ensuring your piglets retain good health. This is achieved via nutrition and utilizing the various vaccinations that "trigger" your pig's immune system into action. The latter enables the system to identify and attack those organisms which are especially virulent.

The following are ways in which pathogens are able to colonize in large numbers.

1. When hygiene is not maintained to a high standard.

2. When infected or carrier pigs are brought into contact with your pet or stock.

3. When you introduce a pathogen and are not maintaining adequate hygiene in husbandry techniques.

4. When you fail to protect your pets with appropriate vaccinations.

5. When you place a piglet or adult in a stress situation.

6. When you overcrowd stock.

7. When breeding accommodations do not meet the standards needed.

8 When you fail, or are slow, to act having recognized your pet is unwell.

Although preventative

husbandry applies to all pet owners, it is the stock of breeders that is clearly at the most risk to the effects of disease. The greater the number of animals kept within close proximity, the greater the opportunity for pathogens to become established, therefore the greater the need to avoid costly vet bills and loss of stock.

manure or garden cuttings are a very dangerous source of both mold and bacteria.

All feeding utensils should be thoroughly washed each day. They should also be returned to the same pens they came from. Replace any appliances that become chipped or cracked. Always wash your hands after handling sick pigs, and before handling piglets. The wearing

This is very important if they are known to be pig owners. Wear a nylon overall when working around your pigs. Such clothing is much less liable to harbor parasites than is regular clothing.

Sterilize all piglet hand feeding utensils after and before each use. These are a prime source of bacteria gaining entrance to your youngster's intestines, and via these to all internal organs. Be sure to hose all pens at least once every week, and remove all fecal matter daily. Do not forget to hose and disinfect any bars used in the piggery. These can be a means of transferring germs from one pig to another as they rub their snouts on the bars.

If your pot-belly is an exhibition pet, always carefully wash down the traveling crate after each use in order to destroy any bacteria that might have been picked up at a show or en route to this. Remember, you can never know when and where pathogens might be present so you must always assume they are everywhere you or your pigs are at.

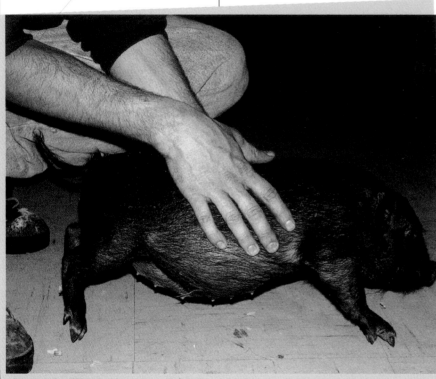

A pot-bellied pig should have at least five evenly spaced teats on each side.

HYGIENE

This clearly embraces every facet of husbandry. All foods must be fresh and stored in a cool dry place that is not exposed to vermin or other forms of contamination. Mold is especially a source of disease. Not only must food be free of this, but it should not be present in the stock accommodations, nor any outdoor pens or exercise areas. Be aware that piles of

of rubber, or disposable surgical gloves is recommended. Likewise, rubber boots are easily disinfected. It is a good idea to step into a shallow bowl of disinfectant each time you enter your breeding area. Have visitors do likewise. It is actually better to restrict visitors near your breeding area because they might introduce parasites or pathogens on their clothing.

QUARANTINE

Any breeder who does not quarantine additional stock is taking an unnecessary risk, irrespective of the source of that stock and what health certificates came with it. Health certificates tell you a pig was healthy at the time of examination, but it just might have been exposed to pathogens after the check up, or en route to your establishment. It would also be wise to quarantine a sow returning from being mated. For newly acquired pigs a quarantine period of 21 days is suggested. It can be used to carefully monitor the diet of the newcomer, and to routinely treat it for parasites and maybe worms as well.

Quarantine provides a reasonable span of time for any incubating disease to manifest itself. At the same time it exposes the newcomer to the local bacteria that will be somewhat unique to your own area. Once the 21 days are over you should house the newcomer near to your existing stock without it being in direct contact with them. This allows the build up of proximal exposure to be accomplished in a well structured manner. Be sure to carefully sanitize the quarantine quarters after and before each use.

VACCINATIONS

There are a number of diseases for which vaccines are available specifically for pigs, with one or two others that were developed for other animals, but which may be used in an extra label manner for porcines. The effectiveness of available vaccines does vary and for this reason not all of them will necessarily be advised by every veterinarian. Further, your situation and location may also be influential in determining which diseases should be protected against. For example, a disease may be especially prevalent in your locality at a given time. If you are an exhibitor or breeder, your stock will be at much greater risk than that of a stay at home pet owner. Certain vaccinations are obligatory for breeding stock, or those transported interstate or country.

We should not overlook the fact that excessive vaccinations can stress a pig, thus could be counterproductive in some instances. All of this suggests that your best course of action is to discuss a program of inoculations with your vet and which is appropriate to your particular piglet's needs. But do ensure your piglet is adequately protected. A number of the vaccinations can be done with a single

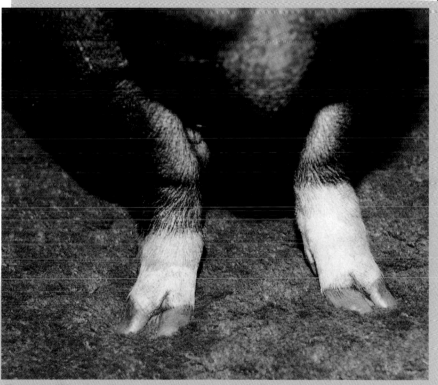

Regularly check your pig's hooves for signs of damage. On average, the hooves will need a trimming about once a year. Your vet can do this for you.

injection. The following summarizes the present major disease-vaccine situation.

Atrophic rhinitis: Respiratory disease. Symptoms include sneezing, runny eyes and nose, abnormal development of snout. Piglets of three weeks and over are especially

susceptible to this disease, the severity being related to the health status of the sow, and the immunity she passes to her offspring. Poor ventilation and hygiene will greatly accelerate this disease and quickly spread it to other piglets. The effectiveness of present vaccines is debatable, but are available to piglets as young as seven days of age. There are numerous other diseases of the respiratory tract, so accurate veterinary diagnosis is essential. Prevention is very much the key word for respiratory problems.

Gastro-Intestinal Diseases: This group of diseases includes *Escherichia coli, Clostridium, Salmonella, Eirmeria, Candida, Coronavirus* and

The folds of skin on the head can be a hiding place for numerous parasites. Be sure to keep them clean.

Transmissible Gastro-Enteritis (TGE). Highly contagious. Symptoms are numerous but will all display diarrhea. Vaccinations are available for certain of this group, for example TGE. Effectiveness is variable. Scrupulous hygiene is the best method of prevention.

Leptospirosis: Contagious. Symptoms include weight loss, circling, reproductive reduction or failure, hemorrhage. Found in water (commonly) and food (less frequently) that has been contaminated by porcine, rodent or cattle urine. Treated pig may pass the causal pathogens for up to one year. The disease is zoonotic (can be passed to humans) so vaccination is mandatory. First piglet vaccination at 4-6 weeks of age.

Porcine Parvovirus: Symptoms are mummified fetuses and other reproductive problems. This is a disease of the reproductive tract. Prebreeding vaccination of sows is obligatory.

Pseudorabies: This is a viral disease of the nervous system. Symptoms include trembling, incoherent movements, sneezing, coughing and weight loss (anorexia). Often fatal in young piglets but rarely so in adults. Contagious to pigs and other livestock, often proving fatal in the latter. Breeding stock should be tested quarterly and tested negative before purchase or being bred. Vaccination if possible, but is prohibited in some states due to its effect on accurate blood testing. Pigs testing positive may have to be destroyed. Avoid contact with regular farmyard pigs which would increase the exposure risk.

Rabies: A disease of the nervous system that is more commonly associated with dogs and wild mammals. Not applicable to pig owners in Great Britain, Australia, New

Zealand, Hawaii and a number of island countries where it has been eradicated, and where stringent quarantine laws have been enacted to ensure it stays that way. No porcine vaccine, but those for other animals may be used in extra label manner based on your vet's advice.

Swine Erysipilas: Highly contagious. Symptoms include lesions, arthritis and blood diseases. Resists commonly used disinfectants, but is killed by caustic soda and hypochlorites (weak acid solutions of chlorine oxides). Recovered pigs may be carriers for life. The causal pathogen lives in soil, water and rotting organic matter, so attention should be applied to these where pigs are pastured. First vaccination at 4-6 weeks.

Tetanus: A disease of the nervous system caused by organisms of the genus *Clostridium*. Symptoms include muscular spasms, arching of the back and lack of balance—which may result in the pig falling over. The causal agents are found in the soil, often that which is contaminated with fecal matter. They enter the pig's body via lesions—such as wounds, scratches or those created by surgery (neutering, spaying and so forth). Hygiene is crucial, as is land management and the treating of minor wounds, especially to stock that has pasture access. Vaccinate according to veterinary advice as the disease is more prevalent in some areas than in others.

STRESS

Stress is undoubtedly the greatest single precursor of disease in all animals. The reason is that it drains nervous energy and in so doing dramatically reduces the mobility powers of the immune system. Unfortunately, it is not always possible to recognize the condition because it displays no obvious outward signs,

The dry food that you feed your pig must be specially formulated for pot-bellies. A good diet will be reflected in your pot-belly's overall appearance.

other than possibly through aggression, depression and similar behavioral patterns.

Stressful situations are, however, easily recognized and among these are overcrowding, close proximity to aggressive cohabitants, excessive heat and cold, lack of fulfilling nutrition, fear derived from the closeness of other animals even though they pose no direct threat, fear derived from an owner's inconsistent behavior towards the pig, excessive noise, and frustration derived from an inability to engage in mating when members of the opposite sex are close by but never available to a given entire (sexually complete) boar or sow. The means of overcoming the various sources of stress are obvious by the the nature of the source itself.

Never underestimate the potential problems created by stress in the well being of your pet. It will directly effect both appetite and a pig's ability to respond to training. I should add that stress can also be caused when an owner is over attentive to a pet that is the sort that does not enjoy excessive fuss. Pigs vary considerably, as do most pets, on this matter. Likewise, a breeder who continually interferes with a sow and her piglets may create stress in the female. This will be transmitted to the piglets. It may manifest itself by the piglets becoming nervous when approached by humans. You must know the nature of your stock on an individual basis.

OVERCROWDING

When you place a large number of pigs in a confined area you obviously increase the risk of disease transmission. Exactly what constitutes overcrowding is not as easy to define as might be thought. It is a subjective topic on which each of us has our own views. Further, it depends on the total environment. For example, it would take only a few pigs to be overcrowded in a piggery that was poorly ventilated, or in which the standards of cleaning were low. The same sized area which was clean, light, and well ventilated might hold more pigs and not represent the same degree of risk. The level of comfort for the pigs would reduce the risk of stress.

The foregoing stated, it would nonetheless be more prudent to divide a large herd into two or more buildings, rather than one large one, in order that the risk of disease spread would be minimized. Each pig should have ample room in which to move about freely without interfering with any other pigs in a given pen.

FAILURE TO RESPOND TO SIGNS OF ILLNESS

A considerable number of diseases, and their spread, could be avoided if all owners were diligent in simple basic husbandry. Often, a condition is seen but is left unattended on the basis that "I will see how things look tomorrow." Unfortunately, and especially where piglets are concerned, tomorrow might be too late. In other instances a minor situation develops into a disease because of secondary infection that proves to be much more dangerous than the original condition. For example, a minor cut left unattended can be the site for all manner of pathogens, which may then proliferate into a killer disease.

In order to respond to a sign of ill health you must of course appreciate what such signs are. The first signs of an impending illness will often be a change in the normal pattern of behavior. A gluttonous feeder (which is most in the case of pigs!) that suddenly shows disinterest in its food, a pig that displays little interest in what is going on around it when it is usually the source of what is going on, or a pig that seems very restless when it is normally the epitome of the term relaxed. Each of these clearly indicates something must be wrong.

Physical signs of ill health will be running eyes or nose, coughing, sneezing, diarrhea, constipation, blood streaked fecal matter or urine, wheezing or other breathing problems, lumps, lesions, lameness, excessive twitching, dog sitting (sitting down like a dog on its rear haunches), vomiting, and excessive scratching and rubbing. Of course, you must be able to distinguish between a temporary condition and one that is prolonged.

Once an infection has been diagnosed, this should prompt you to consider how it got established in your stock. All management practices should be reviewed to prevent the problem happening again. You are strongly advised not to attempt home diagnosis. Most diseases display similar clinical signs. Only microscopy and blood testing can actually determine both the disease and the causal organism and strain of this. Medicines are not always pathogen specific, so unqualified use of these can be dangerous. What the former term means is that medicines will as often kill beneficial bacteria as they will those creating a problem. This means that your pet's exposure time to given compounds is invariably limited if adverse side effects are to be avoided. Only your vet is trained to know what the negatives are when a given medicine is being used. Always follow administration instructions. Do not discontinue a given treatment because your pet seems to have recovered. This may result in a relapse if some of the pathogens have survived— and they will likely be more resistant to the medicine.

PHYSICAL EXAMINATIONS

Part of your husbandry should be a weekly physical examination of each pet or your breeding stock. Apart from the benefits of the exam in itself, it also gets porky used to being handled and checked. Wipe any dirt from the corner of the eyes using tepid water. Inspect the ears for any obnoxious odor or signs of dirt. You can carefully wipe the ear with a mild solution of saline water, or with a preparation from your vet. Try to examine the teeth to see if they are clean and that the gums are in no way swollen.

Check the entire body carefully for any indications of skin problems, such as lesions, lumps or external parasites. Pigs rarely suffer from external parasites, but check in the folds of skin on

the snout, behind the ears, and at the root of the tail, which are the most vulnerable places on these pets. Proprietary treatments will eradicate most such parasites. The most common place where external parasites will live are in the pet's bedding, so be sure this is cleaned each week.

If the tusks are getting long they should be carefully filed down, or surgically removed once the permanent tusks have erupted. This takes place when the pig is about 6-10 months of age.

EYE PROBLEMS

The fact that adult pot-bellied pigs invariably have a number of skin wrinkles around their eyes can result in problems. These may turn the eye lashes inwards which cause them to rub against the surface of the eye. Varying degrees of discomfort are then the result. Sometimes the problem has a genetic base, and this is known as entropion. If this is diagnosed, the pig should not be used for breeding no matter how good it is in other aspects of its conformation. The extent of eye wrinkles is itself genetic. If your pot-belly should display runny eyes but is otherwise in good health take him or her to the vet for examination. The problem can be overcome by surgical removal of some of the skin around the eye, which normally corrects the position of the eyelashes. Failure to attend to this not only subjects your pet to continual pain, but could result in blindness.

HOOF CARE

While the hoof of ungulates

is a very sturdy appendage, it can be the source of many problems if it is not cared for correctly. There is a tendency with pet owners to regard it merely as a hard nail rather like our own, or that of other pets. However, we do not walk on our nails, nor are they so complex in their structure. The pig evolved with five digits but one of these no longer exists. This leaves two large medial claws and two laterals at the back of the feet, which do not touch the floor. The pig walks on the medials so anything that negatively affects these will clearly create lameness.

If the ground that your pet exercises on is natural (soil) and reasonably hard, this will help keep the hoofs in good shape. Artificial floors which have slippery or abrasive surfaces will increase the risk of lameness. Artificial floors have the effect of causing fissures in the hoof wall. Often these are small and may easily be covered by mud, so they are not readily seen. The soft inner part of the hoof becomes infected and creates lameness. Unfortunately, the ideal floor for pigs has not yet been produced, so in every case there is a disadvantage to weigh against its advantage.

Wood is a good surface but is not easily kept clean, nor has it a long life. Concrete is hygienic but often abrasive, to what degree depends on how it was prepared and how long it has been down. Plastic, aluminum, and other slated floors each have good and bad aspects. Fissures created by floor surfaces can be longitudinal or vertical. They give rise to foot rot (septic laminitis). Excessive water loss from the hoof can also result from damage to its exterior wall. This too will cause lameness.

Inadequate diet will also create lameness. If needed constituents are missing (or given in excess), this will result in poor hoof formation making it either too hard and brittle, or too soft. Walking for long periods on dirty wet floors or ground will also predispose a hoof to problems, so in many ways a pig's hoof can be adversely affected under domestic conditions.

Under normal conditions you should only need the hoofs trimmed about every 9-12 months. The type of flooring your pets walk on has a considerable influence on this aspect. You can reduce the risk of small fissures being a problem by applying a hoof oil. This will reduce the effect of water loss from the hoof—but it can also mask fissures, so careful regular inspection of the hoof is essential. A good hand lens is a useful tool to have for this. Between trimmings you can use a file to keep the hoof in good shape, and you can attend the actual trimming yourself if you care to study the subject. Trimming a hoof is the easy part, the difficult bit is doing this to the correct extent and angles. The wall of the hoof protects a very delicate and soft internal structure which can easily bleed and cause pain if too much of the wall is removed.

WORMS

Many species of worms live in your pig, but most cause little problem: some are actually beneficial. The real problems come from those which are parasitic and which infest their host to the degree that they deny it benefit from the food it eats. Roundworm and tapeworms, which live in the intestinal tract, are the two most well known, but others can live in the lungs, heart and other organs. You should routinely deworm all your stock.

Piglets can be attended to at four weeks of age, with a repeat dose three weeks later. Breeding sows should be dewormed before being bred. There are various methods of administering anthelmintics and these include injection (those which are highly soluble), by paste (given orally), or by being given in the pig's food. Because you have no control over dosage, when compared to the alternatives, administration through a pig's food is not the most favored method.

Anthelmintics are much improved over those of past years and have a broad spectrum of activity and a wide safety margin. Those, such as the benzimidazoles are now the most widely used. Sustained release preparations will likely become more used in the future because these overcome the need for repeat dosing. They remain active over a longer period in the gastro-intestinal tract. Given the very extensive range of deworming formulations now on the market, you should discuss these with your veterinarian who will no doubt have a favored choice.

If they are given the proper care, pot-bellies are essentially very healthy animals. Good husbandry is a must for keeping a pig in sound condition.

The extent of hair on a pot-belly is minimal. It can vary in length on an individual basis.

MISCELLANEOUS HEALTH MATTERS

Wounds: These will commonly arise from fighting, or from cuts caused by sharp projections, such as barbed wire fencing, protruding nails in wood and the similar. The first thing to do is clean the wound using a mild saline solution or a germicidal soap. Next, apply a suitable antiseptic ointment, or a coagulant (obtained from your vet and kept in your first aid box) and dress this with a compression bandage. Once the bandage is soaked do not remove it but simply add more bandage while you hurriedly take the pig to your vet. Minor cuts will of course heal themselves once the bleeding has stopped—but do check that they are healing and are kept clean. Keep the pig in a controlled environment at this time if you are a breeder.

Hypothermia: This is especially dangerous in piglets during the first 48 hours or so of their lives. It is a major cause of death with these pets. A cold piglet will crowd with its siblings and lie closer to its mother, which increases the risk of death by being crushed. It also takes growth energy needs and transfers it to energy used for keeping warm (shivering). This creates what is known as the hypothermia/starvation syndrome. Poorly heated accommodations, incorrect height or faulty, infrared lamps, and exposure to drafts are the main problems to be safeguarded against.

In the event of a chilled piglet, your immediate need is to raise the body temperature by the use of blankets, immersion in warm water (never too hot otherwise the piglet will traumatize), placing in a warm room, on hot water bottles, or other obvious means. If frostbite is apparent or feared, contact you vet immediately. Unless this is severe, no permanent damage will be done.

Heat Stroke: Never leave your pet in a vehicle on a warm or hot day, especially a

Nap time for porkie. When your pig is tired, let it rest undisturbed.

piglet. Those who exhibit pigs are the most likely to be guilty of this problem. Cramp, expressionless (staring) eyes, twitching, vomiting, diarrhea and collapse are the various clinical signs. Remove the patient to a cool shaded spot and apply cold water blankets. This is the most rapid way to bring body temperature down to a safe level. Once the pig is recovering, take it for a check up to the nearest vet as shock may be the next problem.

Bear in mind that your pet does not have a protective coat of hair so is very subject to sunburn. The use of a suitable sun block cream is suggested for pigs exposed for long periods when on an outing (as at an exhibition). This is especially appropriate to white or low pigment colors such as silver. In the event of sunburn, or any other burn, (flame, chemical and so on), cool the area with water or ice pack to alleviate pain, then have the nearest vet treat the burned skin.

Stray Voltage in Accommodations: A large herd that is kept within indoor housing for long periods may display behavioral changes that can be due to electricity used in the housing. This is not the problem in pigs that it is in dairy cattle, for example, because less equipment is used. Nonetheless, if you experience behavior changes, or reproductive reduction in litter size, it is an aspect worthy of mention to your vet when discussing the problem you have noted.

Shock: This will invariably follow an accident, fight, bad wound, poisoning and other causes. The first course of action is to move the patient away from immediate danger (from the road or such) with the least possible disturbance. Use some form of stretcher. Do not let the head go backwards such that blood is swallowed. Treat the most life threatening problem, such as cuts or poison. Next, remove the patient to a quiet spot and cover it with a blanket, or whatever, in order to reduce the risk of hypothermia. Do not overheat the patient. Transport to the nearest vet, or wait for his/her arrival if the vet advises this.

Acknowledgment

This volume in the *Basic Domestic Pet Library* series was researched in part at the Ontario Veterinary college at the University of Guelph in Guelph, Ontario, and was published under the auspice of Dr. Herbert R. Axelrod.

A world-renown scientist, explorer, author, university professor, lecturer, and publisher, Dr. Axelrod is the best-known tropical fish expert in the world and the founder and chairman of T.F.H. Publications, Inc., the largest and most respected publisher of pet literature in the world. He has written 16 definitive texts on Ichthyology (including the bestselling *Handbook of Tropical Aquarium Fishes*), published more than 30 books on individual species of fish for the hobbyist, written hundreds of articles, and discovered hundreds of previously unknown species, six of which have been named after him.

Dr. Axelrod holds a Ph.D and was awarded an Honorary Doctor of Science degree by the University of Guelph, where he is now an adjunct professor in the Department of Zoology. He has served on the American Pet Products Manufacturers Association Board of Governors and is a member of the American Society of Herpetologists and Ichthyologists, the Biometric Society, the New York Zoological Society, the New York Academy of Sciences, the American Fisheries Society, the National Research Council, the National Academy of Sciences, and numerous aquarium societies around the world.

In 1977, Dr. Axelrod was awarded the Smithson Silver Medal for his ichthyological and charitable endeavors by the Smithsonian Institution. A decade later, he was elected an endowment member of the American Museum of Natural History and was named a life member of the James Smithson Society by the Smithsonian Associates' national board. He has donated in excess of $50 million in recent years to the American Museum of National History, the University of Guelph, and other institutions.

INDEX